THESE WERE ACTORS

THE BOOK

THESE WERE ACTORS

Extracts from a Newspaper Cutting Book
1811—1833

SELECTED AND ANNOTATED

by

JAMES AGATE

HUTCHINSON & CO. (Publishers), Ltd.

LONDON : : NEW YORK : : MELBOURNE

TO
JOHN GIELGUD
OUR FIRST PLAYER

Made and printed in Great Britain by
The Camelot Press Ltd., London and Southampton

LIST OF ILLUSTRATIONS

INTRODUCTORY

"WE are pretty safe," wrote William Archer, "in setting down the twenty-five years between 1810 and 1835 as the winter solstice of English drama." The Shakespearian scholar Harness, writing in *Blackwood's Magazine* for June, 1825, asks the question: "Who are your successful authors?" And provides his own answer—"Planché and Arnold, Poole and Kenney; names so ignoble in the world of literature that they had no circulation beyond the green-room." It is an odd circumstance that the period in which the English drama was at its lowest should have been that in which acting and the criticism of acting were at their highest. Was it because there was no contemporary drama to criticise? Was it because the dramatist most frequently acted during those years was Shakespeare? "The greatest artist is he who is greatest in the highest reaches of his art." Lewes's dictum applies equally to the actor and to the critic who discusses him.

I do not feel called upon to debate how well or ill the great critics who flourished in the period under discussion would have fared if they had had to match themselves against the plays of Ibsen, Tchehov and Mr. Shaw, any more than I want to discuss how Mrs. Siddons would have fared if, instead of Mrs. Haller, she had been faced with the rôles of an altogether stranger Mrs. Alving, Madame Ranevsky and Mrs. Warren. It is a mark of futility in playgoers to ask what we should think of the great Sarah's acting if we were to see it to-day. The question is improperly put. What we ought to ask, except that there is no need, is: What should we think of a modern actress whose genius in our day was comparable to that of the Siddons in hers? The intellectual drama was born in this country on the stage of the Royalty Theatre on December 9th, 1892, with the first performance of Mr. Shaw's *Widowers' Houses*; Clement Scott's Newspaper Cutting Book ends fifty-nine years earlier. Now I am content to believe that the contributors to it, had they been born two generations later, would have reorientated their intellects in the matter of this new aspect of playgoing. It is true that Scott himself failed to make head or tail of the new growth; I hope it will not be held ungracious in me to suggest that he was the greatest *dramatic reporter* of all time, and that it is asking too much to insist that he should have been possessed of a first-class critical apparatus as well.

The principal contributors to Clement's Book are Hazlitt and Leigh Hunt; Hazlitt in the *Examiner*, the *Morning Chronicle*, the *Champion* and *The Times*; Leigh Hunt in the *News*, the *Tatler* and the *Examiner*, of which he was Editor. There is much more of Hazlitt than of Hunt in Scott's volume—which henceforward I shall call The Book—and for a reason which will presently be apparent. William Archer tells us that Hunt "was the first writer of any note who made it his business to see and report upon all the principal events of the day. No doubt he had predecessors and contemporaries in the craft; but oblivion has swallowed up not only their writings, but their very names." Not all their names. In my *English Dramatic Critics* I was able to disengage from oblivion Francis Gentleman (1728–84), whose organ was the *Dramatic Censor*, Henry Bates (1745–1824), who contributed to the *Morning Post*, and one John Taylor (1757–1832), also of the *Morning Post*. But let that pass. Broadly speaking, and forgetting about Addison's and Steele's occasional flirtings with the drama, Leigh Hunt was the first dramatic critic. He functioned during two periods separated by an interval of nearly twenty years. According to Archer, he "was the theatrical critic of the *News* from its commencement in May, 1805, until the end of 1807; from January, 1808, until he went to prison in February, 1813, he filled the same office, though with somewhat less assiduity and vehemence, on the staff of his own paper, the *Examiner*. Before leaving prison he announced his intention of 'resuming the theatrical criticism' of the paper, and even wrote and published, during the last six weeks of his durance, a series of *Sketches of the Performers*, male and female, tragic and comic. Very soon after his release he went to see Kean, the new star, as Richard III, and published (February 26, 1815) a criticism in which he confessed himself 'on the whole disappointed,' not finding the actor so natural as Hazlitt's eulogies had led him to expect. After this one paper he did no more for nearly two years, leaving the theatrical criticism to Hazlitt and others. Towards the end of 1816 his signature re-appears once or twice, but he seems to have lost his taste for theatre-going, and his criticisms are few and far between. He was in his single person the whole staff of the *Tatler* (a daily paper) from September 4, 1830, till February 13, 1832." Whereas Hazlitt, beginning to write about the theatres in October, 1813, continued with very little interruption until within two years of his death in 1830.

Now, who is the critic of the *Morning Herald* and the author of the articles on Kean's Hamlet, Kean's Iago, Talma, Grimaldi and the

Return of Kean? Can it be Thomas Noon Talfourd (1795–1854), the famous lawyer, man of letters and friend of Dickens, the "Mr. Sergeant Talfourd, M.P." to whom *The Pickwick Papers* were dedicated? Called to the bar in 1817, he eked out a livelihood by writing theatrical criticisms, whereby he contracted, according to Crabb Robinson, "a style of flashy writing" which he afterwards amended. Discussing Talfourd's essays in general in the *North British Review* for May, 1856, the writer said that there was not one which was not "partially impaired by the flux of words which was Talfourd's bane." Now, the style of the *Morning Herald* critic appears to me to be very much that of Talfourd, and I should have no hesitation in ascribing the articles to him but for the fact that the first two, having to do with Kean's Hamlet and Iago, were written in 1814, when Talfourd was still in his teens. Can their author be Lamb? The use of "hath" for "have" and the phrase "in the saucy jargon of the day" make the conjecture not impossible. As against this, I cannot think that Elia would ever have found it in his heart to write of the wretched Sowerby that he is "certainly the most miserable actor." John Hamilton Reynolds? This young ex-insurance clerk wrote dramatic criticisms, but they were for the *Champion*, a Sunday paper under the editorship of John Scott. Also his earliest article is sometime after April, 1816. The poet Keats, who deputised for Reynolds for a few weeks at Christmas time? But still the paper is the *Champion*, and again the time and the part don't fit. The date of Keats's first professional attendance at the theatre was December 15th, 1817, and on that night Kean appeared as Richard III. My little book, therefore, presents a tiny but first-class literary problem. Who was the *Morning Herald's* considerable and practised critic who on March 14th, 1814, contributed the article on Kean's Hamlet, and on May 9th in the same year the article on Kean's Iago? I must leave it to readers with a better nose than mine to fill in this gap in my scholarship. There are other gaps.

Now about the *News*. The article on Macready's début reads like Hunt. At that date (1816) he had very nearly reached the end of his first period of dramatic criticism. Even so I would accept Hunt as the author, in 1817, of the articles on Mr. Bonner Thornton, Mr. Fisher, and possibly of that on Miss Smithson, the lady whom Berlioz afterwards married. The accounts in the *News* of the Kean rows and the Crazy Nights at Covent Garden and the Lane, in the *Morning Chronicle* of the Poole *v.* Elliston trial, in the *Morning Herald* of the Royal visits to the theatre and the Retirement of Kean are,

I suggest, the work of reporters. And the fate of reporters is to be anonymous. The account of the Spectacles at Covent Garden and Drury Lane? I have been unable to discover who wrote these. Last in this table of blanks, let me admit to being completely baffled by the initials, P. G. P.

I shall be asked what use it is—I had rather the question had run, what pleasure—to us to-day to know how Kean played this part, and Macready that. Coupled with this will be the demand to know how far one can be sure that the performances were as their critic described them. Are not Kean's Shylock, Othello, Lear those parts plus something Hazlitt brings to them? Yes. But suppose we take another critic's opinion on the same performance, compare the two, and see whether something common does not disengage itself. If two astronomers telephone to the papers that they have beheld a new star, I am satisfied that a new star has been discovered. I do not wait for a third astronomer to add his confirmation. I ask the reader to compare accounts of Macready's Macbeth. The first is from Hazlitt:

> Mr. Macready sees no dim, portentous visions in his mind's eye; his acting has no shadowy landscape back-ground to surround it; he is not waited on by spirits of the deep or of the air; neither fate nor metaphysical aid are in league with him; he is prompter to himself, and treads within the circle of the human heart. The machinery in *Macbeth* is so far lost upon him: there is no secret correspondence between him and the Weird Sisters. The poet has put a fruitless sceptre in his hand—a curtain is between him and the "air-drawn dagger with its gouts of blood"; he does not cower under the traditions of the age, or startle at "thick-coming fancies." He is more like a man debating the reality, or questioning the power of the grotesque and unimaginable forms that hover round him, than one hurried away by his credulous hopes, or shrinking from intolerable fears. There is not a weight of superstitious terror loading the atmosphere and hanging over the stage when Mr. Macready plays the part. He has cast the cumbrous slough of Gothic tragedy, and comes out a mere modern, agitated by common means and intelligible motives. The preternatural agency is no more than an accompaniment, the pretended occasion, not the indispensable and all-powerful cause. It appears to us then, that this excellent and able actor *struck short* of the higher and imaginative part of the

looking vagabond Kean never improved in anything. In some things he could not, and in others he would not.

Or the compendiousness of the same critic's:

Mr. Meggett has played Octavian twice at this theatre. He is a very decent, disagreeable actor, of the second or third-rate, who takes a great deal of pains to do ill. He did not, however, deserve to be hissed, and he only deserves to be applauded, because he was hissed undeservedly.

Have we not exchanged the dimension of use for that of pleasure? But we must begin our extracts. It is June, 1812, and Mrs. Siddons has decided that though there may be no end to her nose there shall be one to her career. Hazlitt's essay containing the purple passage about the idol not only hushing the tumultuous shouts of the pit and quenching the blaze of surrounding beauty, but possessing a face appearing to the lonely student like an eye from heaven and a voice to awaken, trumpet-wise, the sleeping and the dead—this was not written until four years later. Our first extract is taken from The Book's third page.

THE BOOK

MRS. SIDDONS

EXAMINER, *July 5th*, 1812 [Hunt]

Mrs. Siddons began her career, we believe, with comedy, or even with opera; but having no comic or vocal powers, she soon found her footing upon what was destined to become her exclusive ground as a female performer—that of lofty tragedy. It is out of our power to compare her with former celebrated and rival actresses, whom we have never seen; but if any of them excelled her in certain characters, the public must form to itself a nobler idea of a stage than any which it is accustomed to entertain. Her *Queen Katharine, Constance,* and *Lady Macbeth,* were almost perfect pieces of acting,—the first perhaps completely perfect, though of a less striking nature than the others. The sleep-walking scene in the last has been much and deservedly admired; the deathlike stare of her countenance, while the body was in motion, was sublime; and the anxious whispering with which she made her exit, as if beckoning her husband to bed, took the audience along with her into the silent and dreaming horror of her retirement; but we know not whether in attempting a natural monotony of gesture she did not throw too great an air of indolence over the scene in general, and whether in particular the dribbling and domestic familiarity with which she poured the water on her hands and slid them over each other, was not even unnatural in a person so situated;—we are aware, that in every species of passion a sublime effect is producible by the occasional mixture of everyday action with strong feeling, but in the instance before us the character is one of violence; and after a general wash of the hands, the poet seems to have marked out the signal and decided action with which *Lady Macbeth* aims continually at the "*damned spot.*" Her finest passages in this character appear to have been those of the scene before the murder and the dismissal of the guests, the latter of which she performed with a finished royalty. The performance of *Constance* was unexceptionable; and here her lofty indignation came into play with all its nobleness in the scene with the Cardinal: her performance of this part also, the violence of which is such a provocation to the noise of inferior actresses,

set a fine example of majestic excess, and was even clamorous
without losing its dignity. But it was in _Queen Katharine_ that this
dignity was seen in all its perfection; never was lofty grief so
equally kept up, never a good conscience so nobly prepared, never
a dying heart so royal and so considerate to the last. That was a
beautiful touch, with which she used to have her chair and
cushions changed, during the wearisome pain of her resting body!
And her cheek too against the pillow! We could almost as soon
forget the grand and melancholy composure of its parting despair,
as the gentler meekness of that of _Clarissa Harlowe_ with the dying
tinge in it,—that dying cheek, virgin in spite of the despoiler. In
considering these performances of her loftier tragedy, it will be
found, we think, that although there was no passion in the range
of that loftiness, which Mrs. Siddons could not finely pourtray,
the predominant feature of her excellence, and that which gave
a cast to its whole aspect, was a certain regality and conscious
dignity, which exalted her powers in proportion to the rank and
supposed consequence of her characters. What she failed in
particularly, was the meekness or humility opposed to this
general feature, including every species of gentler tenderness,
especially that of love. Her _Belvidera_, for instance, was excellent
where she had to complain of wrong or to resent injustice, but
little less than distasteful in the amatory part of it. This deficiency
she partook with her brother John; but while she resembled him
in this respect, as well as in the singular advantages of his person
and the dignity of his aspect, she was in everything else as much
his superior as nature is to art, or as a fine, unaffected, and deep-
toned picture, is to one full of hard outlines, stiff attitudes, and
coldness of colour. The worst thing an ambitious actor has to
contemplate is the want of something to leave behind him, that
shall carry down an idea of his talents to posterity; and if he makes
use of the beauties of those that have preceded him, he is rewarded
with the mortifying consciousness that all which survives of him
will in like manner become the portion and the display of others.
What was original, for instance, with Garrick, is confounded
with what has descended from him to living actors; and what may
be original with them will be lost in the imitation of their suc-
cessors. The painter and writer are their only resource against
absolute oblivion: and like Garrick, Mrs. Siddons has fortunately
wanted neither. Her portrait, as the tragic _Muse_, by Sir Joshua
Reynolds, will perpetuate the lofty character of her power, and

her possession of the theatrical throne: and among the small number of happy compliments, will never be forgotten the one paid her by Dr. Johnson, when he could not find her a chair in his room—"Wherever you appear, Madam, you see there are no seats to be had."

The great Sarah belonged to the order of people who will not be told, which was how she came to play Rosalind. This was dreadfully received. The tragédienne is said to have strutted about the stage like Lady Macbeth or Belvidera. She was supposed to be acting comedy and did not. Did the audience laugh? No. Were they diverted? No. They admired the extraordinary refinement of the actress, and that was all. John Taylor has left us an account of her costume on this occasion: "It was not that of either man or woman. Her Hussar boots with a gardener's apron and petticoat behind, gave her a most equivocal appearance, which rendered Orlando's stupidity astonishing, in not making a premature discovery of his mistress. What caused Mrs. Siddons to innovate upon the former representations of this character in the article of dress we cannot guess; but we are certain that she could not appear to less advantage in any other habiliment whatever."

Mrs. Siddons made several appearances subsequent to her retirement; they were mostly in support of her family. Of an appearance as Lady Macbeth in 1817 Hazlitt wrote: "We thought her performance the other night inferior to what it used to be. She speaks too slow, and her manner has not that decided, sweeping majesty, which used to characterise her as the Muse of Tragedy herself. Something of apparent indecision is perhaps attributable to the circumstance of her only acting at present on particular occasions. An actress who appears only once a-year cannot play so well as if she was in the habit of acting once a-week. We wish Mrs. Siddons would either return to the stage, or retire from it altogether. By her present uncertain wavering between public and private life, she may diminish her reputation, while she can add nothing to it." Her last appearance was in 1819 when she played Lady Randolph in Home's *Douglas* for the benefit of Charles Kemble. She died in 1831 at the age of seventy-six.

GEORGE FREDERICK COOKE

Of all the actors who flourished in his time, Lamb declared Bensley to have had "most of the swell of soul," to have been "greatest in the delivery of heroic conceptions, the emotions consequent upon the presentment of a great idea to the fancy." Of all the actors I never saw, Kean included, I feel that George Frederick Cooke had most of the swell of temper. If I had another set of brains and another pair of hands to match, one of my first undertakings would be a Life of Cooke, the Great Irascible. My heart warms to a man who could thrust the whole of his benefit receipts, some four hundred pounds, into the fire before squaring up to a pothouse bully claiming that Cooke had insulted him because he was poor and the great actor rich. What with the spleen and the drink, Cooke spent a good deal of his time behind prison bars; the public welcomed him with open arms on his return. He could give better than he could take; witness the occasion when, on the stage at Liverpool, and called to apologise for some affront, he said: "Apology from George Frederick Cooke! Take it from this. There is not a brick in your infernal city which is not cemented by the blood of slaves."

Not surprising that the contemplative side of Hamlet was lost on one whom Doran calls "this compound of genius and blackguard"; his Prince of Denmark was said to be even worse than that of Henry Siddons. As against this, Cooke was probably the best Hamlet whose skull has posthumously figured in the Graveyard Scene! Let Doran tell. "When Edmund Kean was in America, Bishop Hobart gave permission for the removal of Cooke's body, from the Strangers' vault to the public burial-ground of the parish, where Kean was about to erect a monument to the memory of his ill-fated predecessor. On that occasion, 'tears fell from Kean's eyes in abundance,' says Dr. Francis; but those eyes would have flashed lightning, had Kean been aware that there was a headless trunk beneath the monument; and that, whoever may have been the savage who mutilated the body and stole the head,—that head was in the possession of Dr. Francis! To what purpose it has been turned, this gentleman may tell in his own words. 'A theatrical benefit had been announced at the Park, and *Hamlet* the play. A subordinate of the theatre hurried at a late hour to my office, for a skull. I was compelled to loan the head of my old friend, George Frederick Cooke. Alas, poor Yorick!' "

MRS. SIDDONS AS LADY MACBETH

MRS. SIDDONS, OLD KEMBLE AND HENDERSON
REHEARSING IN THE GREEN ROOM

It was in the autumn of 1810 that Cooke first performed in America. If Mrs. Siddons had adapted her question about chimney pots, "How gat he there?" the answer would have been that he was half persuaded and half kidnapped. Two years of America sufficed to finish off the great actor, who appears to have been magnificent as Richard, Shylock, Iago and Sir Giles Overreach. Hypocrisy was his forte. Here is Leigh Hunt on this actor:

Mr. Cooke is the Machiavel of the modern stage. One would imagine that if he had been in the French theatre during the revolution, when actors became legislators, he might have become the most finished statesman of his day. He can be either a gloomy hypocrite, like Cromwell, or a gay one, such as Chesterfield would have made his own son. He can render all his passions subservient to one passion and one purpose, and can

". . . smile, and smile, and be a villain."

Like most statesmen, however, he can do nothing without artifice. His looks and his tones invariably turn him from the very appearance of virtue. If he wishes to be seriously sentimental, he deviates into irony; if he endeavours to appear candid, his manner is so strange and inconsistent that you are merely inclined to guard against him the more. It is for these reasons that his gentlemen in sentimental comedy become so awkward and inefficient, that his Jaques in *As You Like It*, instead of being a moralising enthusiast, is merely a grave scoffer, and that his Macbeth, who ought to be at least a majestic villain, exhibits nothing but a desperate craftiness. Of his Hamlet one would willingly spare the recollection. The most accomplished character on the stage is converted into an unpolished, obstinate, sarcastic madman.

Mr. Cooke is, in fact, master of every species of hypocrisy; and if he is a confined actor, it must be confessed that his powers are always active and vigorous in their confinement. He is great in the hypocrisy that endeavours to conceal itself by seriousness, as in Iago and Stukely in Edward Moore's *The Gamester*, in the hypocrisy that endeavours to conceal itself by gaiety and sarcasm, as in Sir Archy M'Sarcasm in Macklin's *Love à la Mode* and lastly in the most impudent hypocrisy, such as that of Richard the Third and Sir Pertinax M'Sycophant in Macklin's *The Man of the World*.
C

Doran relates how once, when playing Sir Archy M'Sarcasm, Cooke forgot his name, called himself Sir Pertinax M'Sycophant, and was corrected by a purist in the gallery. Cooke looked up, and happily enough remarked, "Eet's aw ane blude!" Strictly speaking, Cooke is outside our period. He died at the age of fifty-six, and The Book has this note:

On Saturday morning, Sept. 26, took leave of this worldly stage, George Frederick Cooke, in the 57th year of his age. The celebrity of this universally excellent player has received the approbation of all ranks and countries, in so public and extensive a manner, as to bid defiance to eulogium. We need only remark, that "*The Man of the World*" has quitted it for ever, *Sir John* now feigns not the sleep of death, and there may he in quiet lie till the last act, when "Richard will be himself again."

The following account of the last days of this celebrated actor is given in a morning paper. If true, it is disgraceful to the country in which he died:

"After wandering from New York to Boston, and Baltimore, and Charleston, he was arrested for debt by some of those persons at whose baneful solicitation he had thrown his country behind him, and became a vagabond in principle and a pauper in fact! This ill-starred and unhappy man, died, as we have been informed, in the rules of the debtor's prison, at York, in which he had been confined for the penalty of a bond, which had been exacted from him in a moment of intemperance, and he paid the forfeit of its fraudful tenour with his life! Thus gloomily was terminated the mortal career of GEORGE FREDERICK COOKE, who was, indisputably, the best inartificial actor that we have seen on the stage of any country."

THE GREATEST ENGLISH ACTOR

With the Siddons in retirement, Cooke in his grave, and John Philip Kemble on his last legs, the stage now waits for one even greater. "No doubt," wrote C. E. Montague, "everything felt pretty much the same as usual to Rachel on the night when a shy, fiery-eyed, little school-marm, who was to make her immortal, strayed into the house." If Rachel was fortunate in having to play to Charlotte Brontë, Edmund Kean was thrice happy that the greatest of English it perfectly consistent with a high degree of admiration of this extraordinary actor, to suppose that he might have carried an ingenious and original idea of the character to a paradoxical extreme. In some respects, your Correspondent seems to have mistaken what I had said; for he observes that I have entered into an analysis to show "that Iago is a malignant being, who hates his fellow-creatures, and doats on mischief and crime as the best means of annoying the objects of his hate." Now this is the very reverse of what I intended to show: for so far from thinking that Iago is "a ruffian or a savage, who pursues wickedness for its own sake," I am ready to allow that he is a pleasant amusing sort of gentleman, but with an over-activity of mind that is dangerous to himself and others; that so far from hating his fellow-creatures, he is perfectly regardless of them, except as they may afford him food for the exercise of his spleen, and that "he doats on mischief and crime," not "as the best means of annoying the objects of his hate," but as necessary to keep himself in that strong state of excitement which his natural constitution requires, or, to express it proverbially, in *perpetual hot water*. Iago is a man who will not suffer himself or any one else to be at rest; he has an insatiable craving after action, and action of the most violent kind. His conduct and motives require some explanation; but they cannot be accounted for from his interest or his passions—his love of himself, his hatred of those who are the objects of his persecution; these are both of them only the occasional pretext for his cruelty, and are in fact both of them subservient to his love of power and mischievous irritability. I repeat, that I consider this sort of un-principled self-will as a very different thing from common malignity; but I conceive it is also just as remote from indifference or levity. In one word, the malice of Iago is not *personal*, but *intellectual*. Mr. Kean very properly got rid of the brutal ferocity which had been considered as the principle of the character, and then left it without any principle at all. He has mistaken the want of moral feeling, which is inseparable from the part, for con-stitutional ease and general indifference, which are just as in-compatible with it. Mr. Kean's idea seems to have been, that the most perfect callousness ought to accompany the utmost degree of inhumanity; and so far as relates to callousness to moral considerations, this is true; but that is not the question. If our Ancient had no other object or principle of action but his in-difference to the feeling of others, he gives himself a great deal of trouble to no purpose. If he has nothing else to set him in motion, he had much better remain quiet than be broken on the rack. Mere carelessness and gaiety, then, do not account for the character. But Mr. Kean acted it with nearly the same easy air with which Mr. Braham sings a song in an opera, or with which a comic actor delivers a side-speech in an after-piece.

But the character of Iago, says your Correspondent, has nothing to do with the manner of acting it. We are to look to the business of the play. Is this then so very pleasant, or is the part which Iago undertakes and executes the perfection of easy comedy? I should conceive quite the contrary. The rest of what your Correspondent says on this subject is "ingenious but not convincing." It amounts to this, that Iago is a hypocrite, and that a hypocrite should always be gay. This must depend upon circumstances. Tartuffe was a hypocrite yet he was not gay: Joseph Surface was a hypocrite, but grave and plausible: Blifil was a hypocrite, but cold, formal and reserved. The hypocrite is naturally grave, that is, thoughtful and dissatisfied with things as they are, plotting doubtful schemes for his own advancement and the ruin of others, studying for far-fetched evasions, double-minded and double-faced. Now all this is an effort, and one that is often attended with disagreeable consequences; and it seems more in character that a man whose invention is thus kept on the rack, and his feelings under painful restraint, should rather strive to hide the wrinkle rising on his brow, and the malice at his heart, under an honest concern for his friend, or the serene and regulated smile of steady virtue, than that he should wear the light-hearted look and easy gaiety of thoughtless constitutional good humour. The presumption therefore is not in favour of the lively, laughing, comic mien of hypocrisy. Gravity is its most obvious resource, and, with submission, it is quite as effectual a one. But it seems, that if Iago had worn this tremendous mask, "the gay and idle world would have had nothing to do with him." Why, indeed, if he had only intended to figure at a carnival or a ridotto, to dance with the women or drink with the men, this objection might be very true. But Iago has a different scene to act in, and has other thoughts in his contemplation. One would suppose that Othello contained no other adventures than those which are to be met with in Anstey's Bath Guide, or in one of Miss Burney's novels. The smooth smiling surface of the world of fashion is not the element he delights to move in: he is the busy meddling fiend "who rides

MISS O'NEILL AS JULIET

MISS FANNY KEMBLE

in the whirlwind, and directs the storm," triumphing over the scattered wrecks, and listening to the shrieks of death. I cannot help thinking that Mr. Kean's Iago must be wrong, for it seems to have abstracted your Correspondent entirely from the subject of the play. Indeed it is one great truth of Mr. Kean's powers, but which at the same time blinds the audience to his defects, that they think of little else in any play but of the parts he acts. "What! a gallant Venetian turned into a musty philosopher! Go away, and beg the reversion of Diogenes' tub! Go away, the coxcomb Roderigo will think you mighty dull, and will answer your requests for money with a yawn; the cheerful spirited Cassio will choose some pleasanter companion to sing with over his cups; the fiery Othello will fear lest his philosophic Ancient will be less valourously incautious in the day of battle, and that he will not storm a fort with the usual uncalculating intrepidity!" Now the coxcomb Roderigo would probably have answered his demands for money with a yawn, though he had been ever so facetious a companion, if he had not thought him useful to his affairs. He employs him as a man of business, as a dexterous, cunning, plotting rogue, who is to betray his master and debauch his wife, an occupation for which his good humour or apparent want of thought would not particularly qualify him. An accomplice in knavery ought always to be a solemn rogue, and withal a casuist, for he thus becomes our better conscience, and gives a sanction to the roguery. Cassio does not invite Iago to drink with him, but is prevailed upon against his will to join him; and Othello himself owes his misfortunes, in the first instance, to his having repulsed the applications of Iago to be made his lieutenant. He himself affects to be blunt and unmannerly in his conversation with Desdemona. There is no appearance of any cordiality towards him in Othello, nor of his having been a general favourite (for which such persons are not usually liked), nor of his having ever been employed but for his understanding and discretion. He every where owes his success to his intellectual superiority, and not to the pleasantness of his manners. At no time does Othello put implicit confidence in Iago's personal character, but demands his proofs; or where he founds his faith on his integrity, it is from the gravity of his manner; "Therefore these stops of thine fright me the more," etc.

Your Correspondent appeals to the manners of women of the town, to prove that "there is a fascination in an open manner."

D

I do not see what this has to do with Iago. Those who promise to give only pleasure, do not of course put on a melancholy face or ape the tragic muse. The sirens would not lull their victims by the prophetic menaces of the Furies. Iago did not profess to be the harbinger of welcome news. The reference to Milton's Satan and Lovelace is equally misplaced. If Iago had himself endeavoured to seduce Desdemona, the cases would have been parallel. Lovelace had to seduce a virtuous woman to pleasure, by presenting images of pleasure, by fascinating her senses, and by keeping out of sight every appearance of danger or disaster. Iago, on the contrary, shows to Othello that he has "a monster in his thoughts," and it is his object to make him believe this by dumb show, by the knitting of his brows, by stops and starts, &c. before he is willing to commit himself by words. Milton's devil also could only succeed by raising up the most voluptuous and delightful expectations in the mind of Eve, and by himself presenting an example of the divine effects produced by eating of the tree of knowledge. Gloom and gravity were here out of the question. Yet how does Milton describe the behaviour of this arch-hypocrite, when he is about to complete his purpose?

"She scarce had said, though brief, when now more bold
The Tempter, but with shew of zeal and love
To Man, and indignation at his wrong,
New part puts on, and, as to passion moved,
Fluctuates disturb'd, yet comely, and in act
Rais'd, as of some great matter to begin.
As when of old some orator renown'd
In Athens or free Rome, where eloquence
Flourish'd, since mute, to some great cause address'd,
Stood in himself collected, while each part,
Motion, each act, won audience ere the tongue;
Sometimes in highth began, as no delay
Of preface brooking through his zeal of right:
So standing, moving, or to highth upgrown,
The Tempter, all-impassion'd, thus began."

If this impassioned manner was justifiable here, where the serpent had only to persuade Eve to her imagined good, how much more was it proper in Iago, who had to tempt Othello to his damnation? When he hints to Othello that his wife is unfaithful to him—when he tells his proofs, at which Othello swoons, when he advises him to strangle her, and undertakes to despatch Cassio from his zeal in "wronged Othello's service," should he do this with a smiling face, or a face of indifference? If a man drinks or sings with me, he may perhaps drink or sing much in the same manner as Mr. Kean drinks or sings with Roderigo and Cassio: if he bids me good-day, or wishes me a pleasant journey, a frank and careless manner will well become him; but if he assures me that I am on the edge of a precipice, or way-laid by assassins, or that some tremendous evil has befallen me, with the same fascinating gaiety of countenance and manner, I shall be little disposed to credit either his sincerity or friendship or common sense.

Your correspondent accounts for the security and hilarity of Iago, in such circumstances, from his sense of superiority and his certainty of success. First, this is not the account given in the text, which I should prefer to any other authority on the subject. Secondly, if he was quite certain of the success of his experiment, it was not worth the making, for the only provocation to it was the danger and difficulty of the enterprise; and at any rate, whatever were his feelings, the appearance of anxiety and earnestness was necessary to the accomplishment of his purpose. "He should assume a virtue, if he had it not." Besides, the success of his experiment was not of that kind even which has been called negative success, but proved of a very tragical complexion, both to himself and others. I can recollect nothing more to add, without repeating what I have before said, which I am afraid would be to no purpose.

I am, Sir, Your obedient servant,
W. H.

And Hunt replies:

EXAMINER, *September* 18*th*, 1814 [Hunt]

As we are not of the opinion of that celebrated personage, Colley Cibber, that it is necessary to have the last word in a controversy, we should have left the question respecting Mr. Kean's Iago to be decided by our readers without further comment; but we are willing previously to set ourselves right where we think *W. H.* has mistaken us. If indeed our Correspondent does not object to the gay and careless air which Mr. Kean threw over his representation of the "Ancient," then there is no matter of dispute between us, for we were never so senseless as to maintain that the character should be all gaiety from beginning to end.

Had Mr. Kean affected a jaunty toothpick manner when he undertook to murder Cassio, or when he advised Othello to strangle the lovely wife on whom he doted, we should never have condescended to enquire whether his style were right or wrong; all that then would have been at issue would be, whether he were more ignorant or more mad. But Mr. Kean was perfectly solemn in both these passages, nor was such solemnity at all inconsistent with the general ease of his demeanour, unless it is maintained that an open frankness can never, without absurdity, be changed to a serious deportment. We praised this original actor because he had given an appearance of probability to a character which has puzzled many of the readers and hearers of Shakespeare—because, instead of the Saracenic grimness usually adopted, he had personated it with the familiar air of a man of the world. It had struck us that the awful pomposity of preparation both in tone and gesture with which the stage Iagos are accustomed to preface their first address to Othello, must, however startling, have rather excited his contempt or indignation against the speaker than any jealousy against his wife, especially when he finds that nothing comes of it. For let it be recollected, that in the first conversation between the General and the Ancient, Iago merely throws out hints respecting the inconstancy of women; he does not pretend to have an atom of proof against Desdemona, but talks of her in such a manner as a libertine soldier might, without exciting much surprise, be supposed to talk of a young, accomplished, high-born Venetian lady. What he says would not have been heeded by anyone but a proud old soldier, who is tremblingly alive to the smallest circumstance which may cast a slur on his reputation: but Iago knew his man, and what would be sufficient for a first course. He is therefore at first content with insinuations. Like all intellectual, calculating villains, he never throws away any energy; if a lie is necessary, he will utter one: if a murder will further his purposes, he will commit murder: but we cannot agree with W. H. that he perpetrates crime for mere sport or by way of experiment, for we can see nothing in Shakespeare which warrants such a conclusion. W. H. charges us with saying that a hypocrite should always be gay: we said no such thing: we merely endeavoured to shew that gaiety was the mask best suited to the purposes of Iago. The instances of Tartuffe, of Joseph Surface, and of Blifil, have no relation to the present subject. Those three persons were pretenders to extraordinary piety and morality, and gravity with them was not merely a necessary instrument, but was the end and aim of their efforts. Not so with Iago; as far as we can understand him, he does not affect a single morality under the sun: his conversation is licentious, and there is no intimation that his conduct was more correct than his language. He pretends indeed to sincere friendship, and we know that the moralist will say that a profligate man cannot be a good friend: we know also that such persons as associated with Iago were and are less particular, and do not think friendship incompatible with a thousand immoralities. Iago, then, has to assume the part of an honest, friendly fellow—a man entirely sincere and without guile; and we again assert with some confidence, that among soldiers he was more likely to pass for what he pretended to be, by a frank and open manner, than by a stiff, formal solemnity. Our Correspondent says that he affects bluntness: true, because politeness has somehow got the character of insincerity. Bluntness, however, is perfectly consistent with gaiety and cheerfulness of manner.

We had stated that, according to our view of the subject, the question of the propriety or the impropriety of Mr. Kean's personation did not depend on the character of Iago; but on the manner most suited for the success of a man with his designs. W. H., however, does not choose to meet us on this issue, but perpetually recurs to the character as the ground of his opinions. Though we still think that this does not affect the question, we beg to say a few words also on this subject. We will readily allow that our Correspondent, both from his acquaintance with Shakespeare, and from his metaphysical skill, is entitled to much attention on this point: at the same time, he has studied the human mind with too much accuracy not to be aware of the uncertainty of the most ingeniously constructed system: nor will he be uncandid enough to be annoyed, because his infallibility is disputed. Without further preface, we do not agree with him when he says that the malice of Iago is not personal but intellectual, because we think a very contrary conclusion is deducible from the play. He has indeed that pride of intellect which makes him hold all inferior understandings in contempt, and which stimulates his indignation when persons whom he supposes to have less pretentions are preferred before him: but he shews no disposition to vent this general feeling of hatred, except against those who personally and particularly offend him. Why does he wish to plunge Othello in despair and ruin? Not as W. H. says "from his love of power and mischievous irritability," but from the more intelligible and more direct motive of revenge. He had been refused the rank which was the dearest to his heart, and moreover he believed that Othello had abused his bed. Why does he attempt to dispatch Cassio? For a very plain and common reason, because Cassio stood in the way of his preferment, and because he held himself sure of succeeding to his place. Why does he stab Roderigo? For a reason which has brought many a vulgar, unintellectual ruffian to the Old Bailey; because the death of his accomplice would, he imagined, remove all evidence of his guilt. Why does he murder his wife? From an impulse of desperate but not unusual rage, at seeing his whole scheme of villainy detected at the moment that he thought all was secure. Such at least is the account that Shakespeare gives, and we see no cause for an ingenious attempt to account, by abstruse investigation, for that conduct which is sufficiently intelligible from obvious principles. Our Correspondent charges us with wandering from the subject of the play. Has he not himself furnished us with the example, and in his able portrait of "the over active mind dangerous to itself and others, and insatiably craving after action of the most violent kind," was he not delineating some ideal being rather than the Iago of the poet? Perhaps he had some existing character before him: at any rate the picture bears a stronger resemblance to Bonaparte than to Shakespeare's Ancient.

And now no more of Kean for the moment. We shall return to him later on.

BANNISTER'S FAREWELL

As one turns the pages of The Book, it astonishes—if unreasonably—to encounter the names of some of Lamb's Old Actors. Elia began his Essays in 1820, and they were published in 1823, which places within very narrow limits the three Essays: *On Some of the Old Actors*, *On the Artificial Comedy of the Last Century* and *On the Acting of Munden*. (The Essays entitled *The Shade of Elliston* and *Ellistoniana* belong to the second group or *Last Essays*, published in 1833.) Now The Book starts in 1811, which allows a period of some eleven or twelve years for certain of Lamb's Old Actors still

GEORGE FREDERICK COOKE AS RICHARD III

JOHN BANNISTER

"affecting a virtue when he knew he had it not." He seemed throughout to say to his instigators, *You have thrust me into this part, help me out of it, if you can; for you see, I cannot help myself*. We never saw signs of greater poverty, greater imbecility, and decrepitude in Mr. Kemble, or in any other actor: it was Sir Giles in his dotage. It was all "Well, well," and "If you like it, have it so," an indifference and disdain of what was to happen, a nicety about his means, a coldness as to his ends, much gentility and little nature. Was this Sir Giles Overreach? Nothing could be more quaint and out-of-the-way. Mr. Kemble wanted the part to come to him, for he would not go out of himself into the part. He is in fact as shy of committing himself with nature, as a maid is of committing herself with a lover. All the proper forms and ceremonies must be complied with, before "they two can be made one flesh." Mr. Kemble sacrifices too much to decorum. He is chiefly afraid of being contaminated by too close an identity with the characters he represents. This is the greatest vice in an actor, who ought never to *bilk* his part. He endeavours to raise Nature to the dignity of his own person and demeanour, and declines with a graceful smile and a wave of the hand the ordinary services she might do him. We would advise him by all means to shake hands, to hug her close, and be friends, if we did not suspect it was too late—that the lady owing to this coyness has eloped, and is now in the situation of Dame Hellenore among the Satyrs. The outrageousness of the conduct of Sir Giles is only to be excused by the violence of his passions and the turbulence of his character. Mr. Kemble inverted this conception, and attempted to reconcile the character by softening down the actions. He "aggravated the part so, that he would seem like any sucking dove." For example, nothing could exceed the coolness and sang-froid with which he raps Marall on the head with his cane, or spits at Lord Lovell: Lord Foppington himself never did any commonplace indecency more insipidly. The only passage that pleased us, or that really called forth the powers of the actor, was his reproach to Mr. Justice Greedy; "There is some fury in that *Gut*." The indignity of the word called up all the dignity of the actor to meet it, and he guaranteed the word, though "a word of naught," according to the letter and spirit of the convention between them, with a good grace, in the true old English way. Either we mistake all Mr. Kemble's excellences, or they all disqualify him for this part. Sir Giles hath a devil; Mr. Kemble has none. Sir Giles is

E

in a passion; Mr. Kemble is not. Sir Giles has no regard to appearances; Mr. Kemble has. It has been said of the Venus de Medicis, "So stands the statue that enchants the world," the same might have been said of Mr. Kemble. He is the very still life and statuary of the stage; a perfect figure of a man; a petrifaction of sentiment, that heaves no sigh and sheds no tear; an icicle upon the bust of tragedy. With all his faults, he has powers and faculties which no one else on the stage has; why then does he not avail himself of them, instead of throwing himself upon the charity of criticism? Mr. Kemble has given the public great, incalculable pleasure; and does he know so little of the ingratitude of the world as to trust to their generosity? He must be sent to Coventry—or St. Helena!

MRS. JORDAN

Here is a sad little paragraph:

THE CHAMPION, *July 14th*, 1816

Mrs. Jordan died at St. Cloud on Friday, the fifth ult. Our correspondent from Paris informs us that Mrs. Jordan was buried in the cemetery of St. Cloud. She has resided in the village for some time with great privacy, under the name of Mrs. James. She was buried in a thin shell, stained black, but uncovered with cloth or ornament of any kind. Mr. Thomas Greatorex, an hotel-keeper in Paris, and Mr. William Benshall, statuary, of Mortimer-street, Cavendish-square, were by accident passing, and saw her interred. They were the only Englishmen present.

The former mistress of the Duke of Clarence (afterwards King William IV) died in poverty. But she was not destitute, having a small balance at her bank. Grand-daughter of a poor but respectable Welsh parson, daughter of a gallant Army officer, Dorothy Bland made her first appearance in Dublin under the name of Miss Francis. Having no success, she came over to this country and told Tate Wilkinson she was prepared to act in tragedy, high or low comedy, opera or farce. Her first appearance was as Calista in Rowe's *Fair Penitent*. Tate Wilkinson has left it on record that after the tragedy she sang a song. She now changed her name to Jordan, and going to London refused to play second to Mrs. Siddons. Resolving to be the first in comedy, she appeared as Peggy in *The Country Girl*, Garrick's emasculated version of Wycherley's play, and in quick been considered as one wrapt up in his own moody reflections as in darkness; and, who may only be said to *think aloud*. Mr. Fisher, with an intrepidity truly admirable, gabbled at the audience in his soliloquies, or seemed to chatter in his natural *patois* to some invisible persons on the stage. In Hamlet, there is an everlasting stream of pure poetry—an eternal spring of beautiful images— and the secret charm of the play consists in the happy art with which they are employed in the illustration, as well as the adorn- ment of the profound casuistry of the character. Mr. Fisher gave us Hamlet in flat prose, and shewed a tender anxiety to reduce all its flowing poetry to the level of stagnant water. He put the unfortunate poet's feet out of joint at least a hundred times: and the verse in consequence halted deplorably. Those who can imagine an interminable Alexandrine, or a Hexameter three or four yards long, will have a perfect idea of Mr. Fisher's delivery of the soliloquies; to other readers we can give but a faint notion of Shakespeare, as translated by Mr. Fisher, by quoting that famous distich of Zachary Boyd:

"And was not Pharaoh a saucy Rascal
That would not let the children of Israel, their wives, and
their little ones, their flocks, and their herds, go out into
the wilderness forty days, to eat the Lord's Paschal."

We did not expect that much grace of utterance, or tenderness of feeling, would have been given to those "Fine closes of thought- ful melancholy," of which in this Play there is such a beautiful redundancy; for who looks for melody from a screech owl, or roses in a stone wall; but we really did not imagine that even Mr. Fisher should have suffered that opaque body, his head, to get so completely between him and the light in reading the play, as to lead him to represent Hamlet as a character so utterly insipid, lachrymose, and conceited, as to keep us alternately yawning and laughing in our sleeve throughout the whole performance.

Our readers have no doubt discovered, by this time, many good reasons why the character was never represented in this way before!

And this, equally severe and sound, of Harriet Smithson:

THE NEWS, *January 25th*, 1818 [? Hunt]

On Tuesday evening Miss Smithson, a lady from the Dublin Stage, appeared at this Theatre in the part of Letitia Hardy, in *The Belle's Stratagem*. This character requires that the Actress who assumes it should have feeling, grace, good breeding, wit and versatility. Miss Smithson has only frigidity, awkwardness, vulgarity, want of taste, and a few other qualifications of the same description, to recommend her in the part to our indulgence or applause. We cannot give out words of good augury with regard to this lady's future dramatic attempts—for we really consider her as likely very soon to occupy a place among those forgotten persons whose memories are lying in cold abstraction in the tomb of all the Capulets.—We however must admit, that her sentence may have owed something of its severity to the malignant influences of that unlucky planet which seems to be Lord of the Ascendant over all persons and things attached to Drury Lane Theatre.

The strongest damnatory evidence against the *cast* of this Play, is the Play-Bill, from which we extract, as a *favourable* specimen of its arrangement, that Mrs. Robinson personated *Lady Frances Touchwood*: and Mr. Stanley, *Doricourt!* We would here give our readers a piece of advice, which they will find to be of infinite service to them, in any visits which they may intend to make to Drury Lane Theatre. As the house—except when Mr. Kean performs—is always intolerably *cold*, we would most earnestly suggest to the Ladies, that they should be warmly muffled up in double cloaks—and that they should be specially careful about their *throats* and their *feet*—and we beg that they will be cautious not to *overheat* themselves, by venturing too suddenly into the *open air* on quitting the Theatre. To the Gentlemen it may be sufficient to recommend boots, belchers, and box-coats—though we would hint, that the addition of a bear's skin or two would not be found uncomfortable in the Russian winter of the boxes of Drury Lane. We cannot give the unfortunate *Pittites* any hope of shelter from "the icy wind of Death" which seems to blow from all quarters at once, unless they could be prevailed upon to attire themselves in three or four pair of warm blankets. With a mantle of this description, and by dint of *sitting very close*, the three dozen and a half who *fill* the Pitt, may get a few degrees above the *freezing point*—but this is all we can promise them.

JOSEPH MUNDEN

TALMA AS HAMLET

Inevitably we come back to Kean:

KEAN

GATHERING CLOUDS

In April, 1823, Edmund Kean is writing from Portsmouth to Cooper, stage manager at Drury Lane. He ends the letter:

Portsmouth is pretty well, but it must be a great many *pretty wells* before I can recover the blow inflicted by whores and aldermen.

The alderman was Alderman Cox, and the Cox *v.* Kean divorce case was a cloud on the horizon.

In November of the following year he writes from Belfast to Elliston, the manager of Drury Lane. He ends the letter:

How goes the Theatre? Where are all my women? Tell Newman to get some good brandy against the 15th of January—to drink damnation to whores and aldermen.

THE STORM BREAKS

On January 17th, 1825, the Cox *v.* Kean case was tried before the Lord Chief Justice, and a special jury awarded Alderman Cox £800 damages. *The Times* immediately started a campaign against the actor. Its leading article of January 18th said:

It is of little consequence whether the character of King Richard or Othello be well or ill acted; but it is of importance that public feeling be not shocked, and public decency be not outraged.

A performance of *Richard III* having been announced for January 23rd, Sir Richard Birney, the Bow Street magistrate, acting on a suggestion of Mr. Secretary Peel, called on Elliston to say he was afraid that there would be a serious disturbance if Kean was allowed to play so soon after the trial. Elliston immediately posted off to Croydon, where he found the actor sitting up in bed drinking brandy and water and smoking a cigar, soothed by a broom girl dressed in picturesque attire, and watching a strolling acrobat

F

tumbling over the chairs and tables. Elliston suggested postpone-
ment of the tragedy and Kean told him to do whatever was the 1825
equivalent of boiling his head. He said he wished to face his enemies,
and added: "In the meantime, see how quietly I am living here."
And I reflect that if it had been in Macready's power to utter such a
goguenarderie at such a time and in such a situation, he would have
been a better actor. *The Times*, of course, was furious at the obduracy
and callousness of this profligate mummer and told Kean in so many
words:

> Let him hide himself for a reasonable time: his immediate
> appearance is as great an outrage to decency, as if he were to walk
> naked through the streets at mid-day.

But Kean was not to be swayed. He appeared on the day and at
the hour he had announced, and here is the full account of what
happened. I shall not break up the, to me, extraordinarily exciting
sequence with interruptive comment. What follows tells the story of
Kean's four next London appearances, his visits to Manchester and
Liverpool, his departure for America, his reception at New York,
at Boston, his return to England to find that there was still considerable ground-swell, and the storm's final subsidence.

THE NEWS, *January 30th*, 1825

KEAN'S FIRST APPEARANCE THIS SEASON ON THE BOARDS OF DRURY LANE THEATRE

At a very early hour on Monday evening, all the doors of
Drury Lane Theatre were besieged by a crowd anxious to witness
the appearance of Mr. Kean. Most of the persons assembled,
we noticed, had a purpose in view, and that was to have some fun.
Some of them were evidently partisans of this gentleman, exclaim-
ing, "We'll carry him through." "The public will support him."
"He shan't be crushed." "What's his private life to us?" "He's a
good actor, and that's what we go to see him for."

It was easy to discern on which side these were—the *anti-crim.
cons.* therefore wisely held their tongues.

The Managers, anticipating some opposition to this precious
experiment, made application to the magistrates at Bow Street,
early on Monday morning, for the assistance of a strong party of
the Police *within the house*. This was at first peremptorily refused,

on the ground, that if they chose to make such out of the way experiments, they must take the consequences upon themselves, but, in the course of the day, upon a more earnest entreaty for assistance, their Worships relaxed in their refusal, and two parties of the patrol were allowed to man the lobbies; though they were strictly enjoined by the Magistrates not to interfere, except in case of actual riot. Meanwhile the thick-and-thin worshippers of Mr. Kean were, it is said, beating up for volunteer defenders; he himself dined in the threatre with a party of his own, very jovially, they say. All the doors, as we have above said, were thronged with noisy crowds long before they were opened; the rush, when they were opened, was tremendously tumultuous—to the great benefit of the pick-pockets; in a few minutes the house was crowded to an overflow without any regard to those who had previously taken places; from that time to the drawing up of the curtain, there was a continual roar of "Kean, for ever!" mingled with yells and hisses; and, to the credit of the softer sex be it written, there were not more than some thirty or forty of them in the whole assembly.

Richard The Third was the play chosen for this experiment on public forbearance, and a play more unhappily appropriate to Mr. Kean's late mishap could not have been selected.

It was evident before the curtain rose that the pit was closely packed with men and boys, who seemed to have been sent there solely for the purpose of defending the culprit from the assaults of his enemies.—Long after the door-keepers and money-takers announced that every place in the pit was occupied, great numbers paid for places and pressed in, so as to force into the pit almost double the number of people it is capable of conveniently holding. All the seats near the doors were doubly and trebly occupied, the people standing on the backs of the seats, supporting one another, till the last rested against the boxes, forming a dense mass of two tiers of human beings. All the boxes and galleries were equally crowded; many persons thought themselves fortunate in obtaining a peep through the little glass windows in the box doors, and through partial openings of them many begged earnestly to be permitted to lend their voices to the uproar. Never, certainly, did we see any theatre so crowded; and those who could not find places, seemed resolved to compensate for their disappointment by adding to the noise and riot. Before the play began, and before Mr. Kean made his appearance, the adverse parties seemed to measure their strength, and prepared their throats for battle. We noticed, at a very early period, that there was a sort of organisation preserved: and some persons were silent, or made a loud noise, as they were instructed by signals.

The same system existed in the boxes, and waving of hands or handkerchiefs set a great number of tongues in motion. With such a crowd there was of course nothing but noise and commotion. Before Mr. Kean made his appearance in the second scene, Mr. Young, who has some resemblance to Mr. Kean, was apparently mistaken for him, but received no more of the attention of the audience after his prototype came forward. On Mr. Kean coming on the stage, in the second scene, the tumult became uncontrollable, and was in one instant carried to the highest pitch.

"Off, off," and some hisses were heard; but the majority of voices appeared to cry, "Bravo, bravo! go on, Kean!" "Kean for ever!" and almost the whole of the audience in the pit rose and waved their hats. Nothing could be distinguished but loud and tumultuous applause. From this time till the end of the play, scarcely a word could be heard. We gathered the meaning of one sentence uttered by Mrs. West as Queen Elizabeth, and of two or three sentences pronounced by Mr. Wallack as Earl of Richmond; once, and once only, we heard Mr. Kean's voice, but all the rest was dumb show—a mere pantomime, without the fun of the Clown and of Pantaloon. Mr. Kean came forward on one or two occasions to address the audience, but he could not obtain a hearing.

"Where's your morality, Kean?" "Little Breeches." "Go and take care of Mother Cox." "Off, off," and "Bravo" and "Go on, Kean." "No connivance," and shouts and noises of all kinds, which the two parties made to drown the vociferations of each other, prevented him even from proceeding so far as to speak.

In the scene in which Richard murders King Harry the cries of "Off, off!" were so vehement, that he left the poor King only half killed; and, advancing to the front of the stage, he stood, cap in hand, leaning upon his sword, looking round the house, as who should say—

"I do *suspect* I have done some offence,
That seems disgracious in the city's eye,
And that you come to reprehend my folly."

However, he had no opportunity of saying any thing at all; and a *lady* in the sideboxes having shaken her handkerchief at him in token of *approbation*, he bowed and withdrew as before, in the midst of the most hideous clamour, and without even stopping to put poor King Henry out of his misery by the finishing thrust. In the funeral scene, Lady Anne poured forth her sorrows amidst the storm unheeded; and, as Mr. Kean felt how awkward it would be to court her under such unpleasant circumstances, he once more came forward to address the noisy multitude.—But as his so doing was the signal for still more noise, he clapped his bonnet on his head in a pet, and proceeded to court her in dumb show, amidst shouts of laughter, horrible groanings, hisses, yells and clappings of hands. When he came to that part in which he offers the sword to Lady Anne, some Stentor in the two-shilling gallery roared out, "Stick him! little breeches, stick him!" and away went the Lord Protector in a huff, followed by cries from another strong-lunged Olympian of "Do ye think to cram *crim. con.* down our throats?" and "Bravo, Kean!" a thousand times repeated by the pittites. The scene with the Lord Mayor and Aldermen was another uproarious piece of business—the Keanites applauding it to the very echo, and the anti-*crim.-con.*-ists making the house ring with execrations. And in this way the play—or rather the farce, ended.

There were several rather laughable circumstances occurred in the course of the evening. One brazen-throated fellow made the house ring with bellowings of *Kean for ever—Turn out the Alderman—Turn out the Society for the Suppression of Vice!* Another was heard in the intervals when both parties were laying by; hoarsely uttering, "*All this 'ere row, about that 'ere actor, and a woman not worth* 800 *farthings.*" Two or three other fellows amused themselves with making flags of dirty pocket-handkerchiefs; and some mischievous wag set a rumour afloat that Mr. Alderman Cox was present. An unfortunate Gentleman in a private box was then invested with Aldermanic honours, and having shown by his gestures his disapprobation of Kean, he was assailed with a well-directed fire of oranges and orange-peel by some blackguards in the Pit.

One gentleman in the pit who was rather vociferous against Mr. Kean, and who was therefore attacked by several other persons, defended his proceedings by saying, "he did not want to encourage vice." His opponents said sneeringly, they supposed he belonged to the Society for the Suppression of Vice; and they wished to form a Society for the Suppression of Vindictiveness. Some other persons, who were hissing, were called cornutos, like Alderman Cox, and were told "they came there to protect their very numerous fraternity."

Since the O.P. row of famous memory, we never witnessed anything like the confusion of noises which prevailed upon this occasion. There was also that evidence of system through the whole which characterised the former celebrated tumult. There were, as we have already stated, very few women present. It is to be regretted that there should have been any; but the regret may be diminished by the fact, that those who were present were warm applauders of Kean. Had they been silent spectators, it might have been supposed that they were respectable persons who had inconsiderately ventured to the theatre.—As it was, they made it perfectly clear that they had lost all sense of common decency. One young woman in the front of the dress circle attracted general attention by standing up and waving her hand-kerchief, and by other indications of enthusiasm in favour of the hero of the night. In boldness and energy, indeed, she was rivalled only by a drunken prostitute in the slips, who screamed out jokes about "horned cattle," which might have excited the envy of Mr. Scarlett himself. On the dropping of the curtain "Manager," from the one party, "Kean" from the other, were reiterated with a degree of clamour absolutely deafening. No notice of either demand was, however, taken. Wallack came forward, and, we presume, announced something or other, when, after a brief interval, the "most sweet voices" of the conclamitants, "in hollow murmurs, died away." At the rising of the curtain, to exhibit the second pantomime of the evening, all had subsided; and when we left the theatre on Harlequin's first approach, every one seemed to have discarded all other feelings beyond an interest in the motley hero's evolutions.

And in the same issue:

MR. KEAN'S SECOND APPEARANCE

On Friday, Mr. Kean, as Othello, made his second effort this season; but though the uproar within the house was quite as decided as on Monday, there was no very crowded attendance. The boxes were by no means full; in some instances the front benches only were occupied; and in the dress circle there was not one lady, and only three or four of a certain description were in the tier above. From this it would appear evident, that the production of Mr. Kean under existing circumstances, or the style of his present performances, will not ensure overflowing houses. There were, however, enough in the house to keep up the spirit of discord without intermission—whatever their numbers, their resolution was pretty strong in this particular. The pit was full, but not crowded; the galleries, however, were well attended; and what is remarkable, as compared with Monday, they were active parties in the business of the evening. Long before the rising of the curtain the galleries commenced uproar. Several placards were exhibited from the front of the two-shilling gallery, with divers inscriptions, such as "Kean for ever!" —"Who insults the public? Elliston."—"No cant. No hypocrisy. Kean for ever and ever." "Let Elliston be called on to explain." These aroused friendly and hostile feelings in the various parts of the house; and so loud were the clapping of hands and applaudings, as well as the hissings, hootings, and howlings, that it would be difficult to determine which party had the preponderance. Mr. Kean's opponents were undoubtedly persevering, loud, and decided. The play commenced amidst all this uproar, and the performance was mere dumb show. A large placard was then exhibited from the dress boxes, stating—"Let Mr. Elliston be called upon to explain!" This proposition appeared to receive universal sanction, and Mr. Elliston was loudly called upon to appear. Having approached so near the lamps as almost to burn his feet, he opened the communication he had to make to the audience by a profound bow. A profound silence seemed to be the requital that he sought, but a preposterous uproar was the return he got,—Mr. Elliston bowed a second time—we thought the house would have come down. Still the Manager did not appear satisfied—he placed his hand upon his breast, and looked up and round the house with an imploring countenance, and succeeded in obtaining a third round of applause. Still he did not seem satisfied, and remained on his original ground. Some cried out "Silence" till nothing else could be heard; others said "Kean for ever," and some said nothing. Of this last description was Mr. Elliston, but then he *looked* "unutterable things." After having thus doled out what he considered, under the circumstances, an equitable measure of patience, Mr. Elliston, beckoning forward as he retired the actors, withdrew from the stage, leaving the audience as wise as they were before he came on, as to the nature of his object. The play then proceeded, but all in dumb show, hardly one sentence being distinctly heard, from its commencement to its close. Mr. Kean's appearance was the signal for the most formidable uproar against him. Shouts were heard from the central boxes of the first circle, of "Go wash your face, Kean, but you can never wash your heart clean," and of "Your face is black, but your heart is blacker"; meanwhile a large body occupying one half of the pit, stood up, waving their hats, and shouting, "Kean for ever," whilst those who cried "No Kean" (principally from the boxes) were by no means idle. Othello was evidently subdued; his whole demeanour was humbled; he seemed to dread the storm which he heard raging. He bowed faintly; and proceeded with the character. His presence during the whole evening was the signal for distinguished uproar; and if it ever assumed a still more violent character, it was when he was attending to Desdemona—spurning her—attacking her in the bed—reading the *Letters*, and throwing them from him &c. There he was greeted with *extra* portions of execrations, the virulence of which, the plaudits could neither drown or mitigate. In the third scene, in the first act, a paper was thrown on the stage from the pit, on which was written, "Mr. Kean come forward." The paper was taken up by one of the servants of the Theatre. Mr. Kean did not once attempt to comply with the request, and his address to the Senate was inaudible, and not a sentence was heard till the latter end of the fourth scene in the first act, when the following lines, spoken by Mr. Wallack, as Iago, excited laughter, hisses, and cheering:—"My cause is hearted—thine has no less reason: Let us be conjunctive in our revenge against him: If thou canst cuckold him, thou do'st thyself a pleasure, and me a sport."— Mr. Wallack, in consequence of the noise being so excessive, was unable to hear the cue given, and there were cries of "Off, off!" Mr. Wallack looked very expressively at the audience and said, "Why should I go off?" Loud applause and shouts of "Bravo, Wallack!" succeeded, and many persons called upon him to "go on." Thus the play continued amidst din and uproar to the end. In the course of it, we could not, however, but admire the pertinacity and zeal of Mr. Kean's advocates. A boy with an orange in one hand, and in the other a stick, to the end of which he had tied a red pocket-handkerchief, continued to display his banner, and shout at every moment that he could spare from sucking his orange. A fat woman, of the Cyprian order, in the upper boxes, waved a once-white handkerchief, and clapped, and cried "Bravo!" most indefatigably. Less prominent, but perhaps not less earnest nor less useful, were the services of other partizans who were stationed in the pit, and were evidently there for the first time in their lives. —They wore blanket great coats, which concealed (and perhaps it was so much the better that they did) all the rest of their garments. They seemed to be that active, if not honest, fraterntiy, who usually ply about stage-coaches, and are called *cads*. After the novelty had worn off, these gentlemen seemed to think it a particularly dull piece of business; and during the latter part of the tragedy could hardly be induced to pursue the shouting with which they began. With the falling of the curtain, a short interval of peace ensued, and the wearied belligerents on both sides remained comparatively silent until the pantomime commenced. The cries for "the manager" now became general. Still, however, the pantomime proceeded. At length the call of "Elliston! Elliston!" became so vehement that the manager felt it necessary to make his appearance. He was received by the friends of Mr. Kean with great applause, and with a strong expression of disapprobation by his opponents. After bowing to the audience for several minutes, silence was obtained, when he addressed them to the following effect:—

"Ladies and Gentlemen:—I thank you for the honour of your silence, and I trust you will extend your indulgence to the hearing of a few words—(applause)—and if one word should improperly drop from my mouth, I hope the agitation of my feelings will be accepted as an excuse—(Cries of 'it will!' mingled with applause and calls for silence).—I stand before you as the servant of the public.—('Bravo, Elliston!').—I come to be a peacemaker. (Applause and disapprobation.)—and I flatter myself that what I have to say will not place either Mr. Kean or myself in a worse situation—('That is impossible!' followed by a renewal of the uproar for some minutes). I have throughout this contest stood aloof, aware that your sense of justice would conduct you to a right decision. I have now an opportunity to explain and have no doubt that we shall end in a right understanding.—(A further pause caused by a renewal of the uproar.)—Ladies and Gentlemen, the engagement which Mr. Kean is now endeavouring to fulfil was made last July.—(Partial interruption) Mr. Elliston

(with vehemence)—this is a moment of too much interest for me
to hazard a quibble, or to go nigh a falsehood, and I pledge my
life to the truth of every word I utter.—('Bravo!') I repeat, the
document is in the hands of my Treasurer; it is witnessed, and
it *was* made in July, 1824—(Applause, intermingled with loud
cries of 'Humbug; come to the point, Mister Manager!')—At
that time there was no belief that the question which has lately
agitated the public mind would be brought to a public discussion.
Mr. Kean's engagement was for a specific time, and for a specific
sum, viz.—twenty nights at fifty pounds a night—with certain
gratuitous points on his side, for which upon this and other
occasions, I am as much his debtor as he is mine.—(Applause.)
The engagement was to begin on the 16th of January, and to end
on the 16th of March. My anxiety to meet your patronage, and
Mr. Kean's engagement, both before and after this period, have
caused me, in order that you might have the full benefit of what
your patronage shews to be highly considered by you, to procure
a new play favourable to his peculiar powers.—(Applause and
disapprobation.) Now mark, Ladies and Gentlemen, I wrote to Mr.
Kean in the progress of his provincial tour to know if he would
be ready to enter upon his engagement with me. We acted upon
this occasion as we have always done, as the best friends, mutually
desirous of assisting each other.—He said, he should be ready to
come, but that he foresaw a storm likely to arise out of a trial
then approaching.—Upon this I applied to his Solicitor, and to
all his friends with great earnestness, and the answer which I
received from them all I state upon my honour as an honourable
Gentleman, which I hope I have always shewn myself, (loud
laughing, and shouts of 'Bravo, Elliston') the answer was, that
the discussion was not likely to come on upon the Saturday
preceding the Monday which commenced Mr. Kean's engagement.—(Interruption of a mixed character—'Why was it not
put off?') Mr. Elliston—Because he was advertised (Hear), and
was I, when Mr. Kean was advertised to appear, to have scratched
his name out from the bills? Had I withdrawn his name, I should
have made myself a party against him, which I never will do.
('Bravo, Elliston.') I could not do it as a manager.—(Renewed
interruption.) Now spare my anxiety.—(Laughter and applause.)
I have one point more. I will not use a harsh term by supposing
that this Theatre had enemies; but I will solemnly declare that
neither my own influence, nor any power I may possess in any way,

has been used to create an influence in Mr. Kean's favour.—
(Applause, and 'It is the Times Newspaper has done it all.') I
have literally suspended the Free List, the Public Press only
excepted. Every kind of order has been denied admission, and
no man is here upon my influence.—(Applause.) Mr. Kean,
Ladies and Gentlemen, is in the house, and if you will do him
the honour to hear him—he will attend."

Often as we have been obliged to break the above report of
this speech, it was interrupted much more frequently in the
delivery. After a considerable time had elapsed, in which the
patience of the house broke forth more than once into murmurs,
Mr. Kean appeared, led on the stage by Mr. Elliston. He had
exchanged his tragic habiliments for a plain suit of black, and
appeared in his own proper colours.—The uproar was now at its
highest pitch—and with very considerable difficulty, Mr. Kean
obtained a hearing. Having advanced to the front of the stage,
he spoke as follows:—

"Ladies and Gentlemen.—If you expect from me a vindication
of my own private conduct, I am certainly unable to satisfy you.—
(Applause and disapprobation.) I stand before you the representative of Shakespeare's heroes.—(Much contention between the
parties favouring and disapproving Mr. Kean.) The errors I
have committed have been scanned before a public tribunal; and
—(here the uproar was so great that we could not collect the
termination of the sentence). On the occasion, Ladies and Gentlemen, to which I have alluded, I have withheld circumstances from
delicacy.—(Much laughter, applause and hisses.) If, Ladies and
Gentlemen, I have withheld circumstances from motives of
delicacy (laughter), it was from regard to the feelings of others—
not of myself.—(Clamours of applause, mingled with hisses.) It
appears at this moment that I am a professional victim.—(Laughter.) If this is the work of a hostile press, I shall endeavour with
firmness to withstand it; but if it proceeds from your verdict
and decision, I will at once bow to it, and shall retire with deep
regret, and with a grateful sense of all the favours which your
patronage has hitherto conferred on me."

After the delivery of this speech, which was received by Mr.
Kean's partizans with shouts of applause, Mr. Kean seemed
greatly agitated, even to tears. He staggered to the back of the
stage, and seemed in the act of falling when Mr. Elliston came
forward and led him off.

THE NEWS, *February 6th*, 1825

MR. KEAN'S THIRD APPEARANCE AT DRURY LANE

The uproar on Monday evening when Mr. Kean was to play Sir Giles Overreach in *A New Way to Pay Old Debts*, was nearly as great as on the preceding Friday; and as several *bruisers* made their appearance on the side of Kean, it assumed a more determined character. Whether Mr. Kean played well or ill on this occasion it is impossible to say. Judging by the expressions of his countenance—for during four acts of the play his voice was not to be heard, and only occasionally in the fifth—we should suspect that he was struggling more with his own mortified feelings than adopting the passions of the character. At an early hour the dress circle of the boxes was two-thirds or three-fourths filled, about twelve only being ladies, whose number was not after augmented; and not more than two or three of the appearance usual in that station. The first tier was filled in about the same proportion both in numbers and sex, and the upper boxes were about half full, with certainly not a greater number of *ladies*. The pit was full, and there were about thirty females there. Even the galleries did not seem to exhibit a much larger proportion of the softer sex. In short it was almost as completely a masculine house as during the O.P. row, and the clamour was not much less intolerable. Many placards were hoisted on this occasion. One was placed in the front of the two-shilling gallery, with a quotation from Hamlet. —"If every man had his deserts, who should escape whipping?" A placard, exhibited in the pit, contained these: "Kean has made an apology, and a British audience is satisfied." A third placard was exhibited, with the words—"British liberality and no cant." The uproar, which was very great before, became trebly violent when the curtain rose. The hooting, howling, and hissing; the cries of "Turn him out," "Kean for ever!" "Off, off!" and others which decency will not allow us to "set down," were terrific. The fights were numerous. One individual in the pit, an anti-Keanite, was shamefully beaten by a regular knot of ruffians, armed with sticks. He was forced from his seat, thrown down, and, in that situation repeatedly struck by some of the doughty heroes.

In the dress boxes considerable annoyance was excited by two dandy-looking young gentlemen, with white kid gloves and half-grown whiskers, by the violence of their vociferations of "Bravo!"

and "Kean for ever!" At length two gentlemen in the back seats took the opposite side, and with considerable vigour shouted "Off, off," in which they were soon joined by others. This roused the ire of the applauders in the pit, and the consequence was a discharge of apples and half-sucked oranges in full volley from the applauders, by which two chandeliers were broken. Even halfpence were thrown, and a third chandelier, just over the gentlemen, sustained some damage. Many persons were alarmed —indeed the pit at this time assumed a terrific aspect, such was the uproar and agitation amongst the Pittites. On the stage nothing proceeded, and Mr. Kean endeavoured to arouse a little mercy for the lady's sake,—Miss Smithson, who was playing Margaret. He pointed to her, as if to intimate her agitation, but nought could check the rage of the pit's fury directed towards the obnoxious dress-box. Eventually Mr. Kean led the lady off, when Mr. Elliston appeared on the stage. This did not affect the noise; he endeavoured to gain a hearing, but in vain. He could not even get attention.

As soon as Mr. Elliston came on the stage, he went towards Mr. Kean and took him most cordially by the hand and heartily shook it, looking at the audience at the same time, as if to assure both, that, be the consequence what it might, he should stand by Mr. Kean. This attention from Mr. Elliston was received by Mr. Kean with the return of warm and grateful feeling; and after shaking Mr. Elliston by the hand, Mr. Kean inclined towards the manager's hand and seemed to *kiss* it. These proceedings were loudly applauded, with the exception of the latter part of the ceremony, which seemed to create a mixed feeling. Mr. Elliston then again endeavoured to obtain a hearing, bowing repeatedly to the audience for that purpose, but he had no success. One gentleman in the front of the pit, about its centre, stood on the orchestra—fencing, as if desirous of making a speech to Mr. Elliston. He remained there for some time and was as little successful as Mr. Elliston. Mr. Kean went to the side of the stage, but uproar continued, partly against them and partly against the mal-content box. After some time had elapsed, Mr. Kean went up to Mr. Elliston, who still remained in front of the stage bowing for a hearing, and made some communication to the manager. Mr. Kean then retired back a few paces. Uproar took a new turn. There were next loud calls of "Kean, Kean!" After these demands, Mr. Elliston bowed and left the stage; but Mr. Kean answered the calls by appearing on the stage with Miss Smithson, for the purpose of proceeding with the play. But this would not give satisfaction: the noises of all sorts were more boisterous than ever. Oranges and orange peel were thrown in abundance; and as one orange went very near Mr. Kean, or actually hit him, Mr. Elliston again appeared on the stage, and picking up the orange showed it to the audience, and appeared to ask if it were thrown at Mr. Kean, pointing to that gentleman. Loud noises seemed to intimate "no, no." Then Mr. E. held the orange towards the mal-content box to enquire whether it was thrown at that object. He was given to understand—yes. Mr. Kean and Miss Smithson had remained on the stage, but he once more led her off the stage; and by this time the storm raged furiously against the mal-content box—halfpence &c. in their progress again coming in contact with the already partially demolished chandelier. One of the gentlemen had moved to the front seat of the box. Mr. Elliston went towards him, beckoned him out of the box, and made signs that he wished to see him behind the scenes, or out of the theatre. This pantomime continued for some time, when Mr. Elliston pulled something out of his pocket—it appeared to be a card— and held it at the gentleman. He then left his seat, as if to go to the door which leads to the stage from the dress circle; and Mr. Elliston quickly went to the right wing, and handed to Mr. Gattie the card, or whatever it was, for the gentleman. This business having been dispatched, by the retreat of the sturdy and noisy gentleman, there was some, not much, cessation of noise. Mr. Elliston returned to the front of the stage, and again essayed to address the audience. There were loud and lusty struggles to gain silence, but the uproar seemed to increase rather than to diminish. Mr. E. kept his station, and at last he gained the oppor-tunity of saying, "Ladies and Gentlemen"; but the sound of his voice seemed to drive all parties quite desperate. There was a regular fight at the back of the pit with one person, who was singled out for hissing and hooting, but he kept his station, challenging all around to single contest. He was buffeted about well, but no one accepted the challenge. However, Mr. Elliston perceiving there was no chance of gaining a hearing, retired. Mr. Kean fetched the lady for the third time, and they proceeded, but it was still dumb show. The man in the pit now kept the whole pit occupied; and, though the gallery exclaimed, "Exchange cards, gentlemen, and be quiet," quiet there was none. Another made the best use of some momentary calm—"Well, this is a new way of paying old debts." The uproar continued, especially when Mr. Kean was on the stage, till the fifth act.—The audience then appeared anxious to take some repose, and Sir Giles Overreach then began to exert himself, and, for the first time, his fawning exclamation of "My Nephew!" was heard. Some of the passages were particularly marked by the audience, particularly—

> "My deed, nephew, shall speak for my love;
> What men report, I weigh not."

He uttered it with the most marked emphasis, and his friends loudly applauded it. The advice to his daughter of "Marry first, and lawful pleasure after," excited loud laughter; but the most uproarious merriment was excited by Sir Giles's acclamation, when he thought all his schemes were perfected, "Now all's cocksure." His declaration that "there will be a time and place, cowards, when you shall feel what I dare do," attracted great notice. It was loudly applied, and uproariously applauded by Mr. Kean's friends. The curtain dropped, however, amidst great uproar. Mr. Thompson appeared to announce the next evening's performances, but the audience would not hear him, and there were loud calls of "Kean, Kean!" They continued most boisterously, even long after the commencement of the afterpiece. Mr. Kean, having changed his dress, appeared in black, and eventually presented himself to the audience. He was evidently much subdued. He coldly bowed, and waited for a hearing with unmoved posture; but an immense time elapsed before silence could be procured. It having been obtained, he spoke to the following effect, in tones of desperate agony:

"Ladies and Gentlemen, I have already made as far concession to an English public as an English character ought to do— (uproar and applause). I hope, for the honour of my country, as I shall, in the course of twenty nights, take leave of you" (speaking with amazing emphasis) "for ever"—(much uproar and cries of "no, no, no!") "I hope for the honour of my country, that this persecution will not reach foreign annals." (Tremendous uproar of exclamations.)

We pretend not to explain what Mr. Kean meant by "foreign annals." If his part could claim any advantage this evening it solely proceeded from a number of bruisers, who were evidently in various parts of the house *professionally*. In the course of the evening, a youth, who was expressing his disapprobation of Mr. Kean, was forcibly dragged from the boxes by a person who was said to be the Jew boxer Abraham Belasco. This conduct raised a cry of "shame" on the one side, and a shout of triumph on the other; but we understand that it will form the ground of prosecution.

And in the same issue:

MR. KEAN'S FOURTH APPEARANCE

On Friday Mr. Kean made his appearance in the character of Macbeth, but uproar was still the order of the night. There was not, indeed, in the present instance, anything like the same degree of violent outrage, or unmitigated clamour, as upon the former occasion; but the opponents were evidently more numerous, and the zealous supporters fewer. The former, however, had changed their mode of attack from hissing and hooting, and cries of "Off, off!" to the more galling and mortifying expedients of shouts and laughter, mock applause, protracted Stentorian cries of silence, and deafening echoes of "Turn them out!—turn out all but the Keanites!"—Only thirteen ladies were counted in the dress circle. In this struggle we can see nothing but the destruction of the drama. On the fall of the curtain the cry for "Kean, Kean!" noisily and resolutely persevered in, though but by few voices, detained us for the result. The overture was suffered to be heard, but when the curtain rose for the ballet the clamour became outrageous, and the poor little children who begin the dance were driven off with evident terror. At length Mr. Mercer came forward, and having with great difficulty obtained a partial hearing, apologised for the inability and exhaustion of Mr. Kean, concluding with assuring the audience that he had gone home in his carriage the instant he went off the stage; with which the clamour seemed to be appeased, and the ballet was suffered to proceed.

NEWS, *September 4th,* 1825

MR. KEAN
(*From the Manchester Journal*)

On Saturday evening Mr. Kean made his appearance in Richard II. instead of Richard III., as had been announced. The house,

TALMA AS TALMA

JOHN PHILIP KEMBLE AS CORIOLANUS

with the exception of the lower boxes, was much crowded, but principally by males, there being but a sorry display of "beauty and fashion." Mr. Kean also took the character of *Frederick Baron Willinghurst*, in the afterpiece *Of Age Tomorrow*. When the curtain dropped, a tremendous uproar took place, and cries of "Kean, Kean," accompanied with a loud clapping of hands which continued for several minutes. At length Mr. Kean came forward and addressed the audience to the following effect:—

"It is impossible to withstand so gratifying a call; particularly at a time when the corrupt part of the Press is bribed to ruin my professional reputation. If the Press of this country be allowed to visit the public characters of professional men with the punishment due to their private ones, the arts and sciences of this country will very soon sink into insignificance. I admit that I have been a 'froward child,' but I have repented me of my error— (*tremendous applause*)—and I think it hard that I should receive such unabated and vindictive persecution. I am driven from my native country to which I may probably never return—(*Cries of 'no, no, you shall not go'*). I have ever found Manchester my warmest friends and advocates—(*Loud applause*) and I shall treasure in my exile the grateful remembrance of the kindness I have received at your hands. In reference to the stigma which has been cast upon me as a public character, I would beg my friends to bear in mind, that we are none of us without our faults. In every station of life we find the traces of the corruption of human nature. Even the great Ministers of State have their faults—(*loud applause*)—and if we approach *the foot of the throne* we shall find errors.—(*Loud applause*) I now bid you farewell for ever.—(*Cries of 'No, no—we won't hear that'*). You have my warmest wishes for your welfare and happiness, and I trust that in my pilgrimage should a cloud pass over me, the remembrance of my Manchester friends will operate like a sunbeam and chase away the saddening gloom.— (*Loud applause.*)"

Mr. Kean, we understand, takes his passage for New York in the packet-ship *Canada*, Captain Rogers, which sails on Thursday.

THE NEWS, *September 5th*, 1825

Mr. Kean: This gentleman appears to have become quite furious. His attack on the "base press," and his half-frantic, half-maudlin ebullitions at Manchester, will be seen in another part

G

of our Paper. Yesterday's Country Journals brought us another and a *lower* display; is there yet a "lower deep"? The Liverpool Advertiser states, that after the performances there was a call for Mr. Kean, and, after some little time had elapsed, he made his appearance, and was received with the most enthusiastic applause. He then addressed the audience nearly as follows:—

"I should be lost to every feeling of sensibility, if I did not most respectfully thank you for this expression of kindness. At this moment, when I am about to leave my country, perhaps for ever (loud cries of 'no, no') such an exhibition of your feeling is of particular value to me. Driven as I am from England by the *machination of scoundrels*, by a *combination of ruffians*, who seem determined to destroy me, I receive, on the eve of my departure, the highest gratification from what I now see. No absence, no contumely, no sorrow—none of the numerous indignities to which professional men, in all countries, are obliged to submit— will ever efface from my mind the gratitude I feel to my countrymen."

It shows bad taste, poor spirit, and a questionable cause thus querulously to throw all blame upon the "base press," "ruffians" and "scoundrels"; and yet the "base press" had had nothing more to do with Mr. Kean's real offence and characteristic letters, than it has with Thurtell's murder of Weare, or Fauntleroy's infamously extensive forgeries. And they too threw all blame upon the "base press." Steadiness is not to be expected from Mr. Kean; but we might hope for a little decency from him now:—however, if it please him, he must still "bite against a file." The whole passage is to be found in *Junius*.

MR. KEAN'S RECEPTION IN AMERICA

THE NEWS, *December 10th*, 1825

RIOT AT THE PARK THEATRE

(From the New York Daily Advertiser, November 16, 1825)

On Monday evening, agreeably to public notice, Mr. Kean made his first appearance at the Park Theatre. The boxes on the first and second row had been previously taken by his friends, and early on Monday all the pit tickets were disposed of, and notice placed on the outside of the doors that no tickets could be had.

About an hour before the time of performance, all the avenues leading to the doors were choked up, and the rush to obtain admittance was very great. All parts of the house were crammed long before the curtain rose, and it was evident that it was composed of materials which would not remain quiet. At the commencement of the second scene Mr. Kean appeared, when the shouts of his friends and the hootings of those unfriendly were almost deafening. He bowed and appeared anxious to address the audience: but the tumult was so great that nothing could be heard. Mr. Simpson, the manager, came forward, and with great difficulty was heard to say that Mr. Kean wished to be heard, and that he hoped an American public would not condemn him without a hearing. When he retired the uproar was renewed, and continued throughout the whole five acts to such a degree that Mr. Kean's voice was not heard during the whole performance. He frequently attempted, by his gestures, to address the house, but it was impossible for his friends to obtain for him a hearing. During the piece he was pelted with oranges, apples &c. At the close of the play, he was announced for Wednesday evening, in the character of Othello, amid uproar and tumult.

"To the Editor of the Daily Advertiser.

"Mr. Editor—With oppressed feelings, heart-rending to my friends and triumphant to my enemies, I make an appeal to that country famed for hospitality to the stranger, and mercy to the conquered. Allow me to say, Sir, whatever are my offences, I disclaim any intention of offering anything in the shape of dis-respect towards the inhabitants of New York. They received me from the first with enthusiasm, grateful in *those* hours to my pride —in the *present* to my memory, I cannot recall to my mind any act or thought that did not prompt me to an unfeigned acknow-ledgment of their favours as a public, and profound admiration of the private worth of those circles in which I had the honour of moving.

"That I have committed an error, appears too evident from the all decisive voice of the public; but, surely, it is but justice to the delinquent (whatever may be his enormities) to be allowed to make reparation where the offences were committed. My mis-understandings took place in Boston. To Boston I shall assuredly go, to apologise for my indiscretions.

I visit this country now under different feelings and auspices than on a former occasion. Then I was an ambitious man, and the proud representative of Shakespeare's heroes;—the spark of ambition is extinct; and I merely ask a shelter in which to close my professional and mortal career.

"I give the weapon into the hands of my enemies; if they are brave, they will not turn it against the defenceless.

"EDMUND KEAN.

"Washington, Nov. 15, 1825."

We received the foregoing note last evening, accompanied by a request from the manager of the Park Theatre that it might be inserted in our paper this morning.

The same paper adds,—"If by the remark, 'that he has committed an error appears too evident from the decisive voice of the public,' Mr. Kean alludes to his conduct at Boston, and supposes that to be the ground of the unfavourable reception he has met with here, we have no doubt he labours under a very serious mistake. It is primarily his moral conduct which excites the opposition of so large a portion of the citizens of New York to his appearance on the stage. How far this apology will satisfy the public we pretend not to say."

MR. KEAN'S RECEPTION AT BOSTON

THE NEWS, *January 22nd, 1826*

DESTRUCTION OF THE THEATRE

It may be recollected that Boston was the place where Kean, when in America before, chose to exhibit one of those freaks to which his habits of life, in some degree, render him occasionally liable.—Because there happened on one of the nights he was to perform to be but a thin audience, he insulted those who did attend by refusing to play. This, the Bostonians at the time said, they would never forgive, and they seem now to have acted up to their previous determination.

It is not to be imagined that Kean was not fully aware that, at Boston, he was to meet with an opposition totally distinct from any deviation he might have made from the path of morality. He, therefore, endeavoured to deprecate the enraged multitude by publishing the following letter:—

(From the Boston Sentinel, Dec. 21.)

We have received the following from Mr. Kean:—

"*To the Editor.*

"Sir, I take the liberty of informing the citizens of Boston (through the medium of your Journal) of my arrival, in confidence that liberality and forbearance will gain the ascendance over prejudice and cruelty. That I have erred, I acknowledge; but that I have suffered for my loss of fame and fortune, is too melancholy an illustration. Acting from the impulse of irritation, I certainly was disrespectful to the Boston public; calm deliberation convinces me I was wrong: the first step towards the Throne of Mercy is confession; the hopes we are taught, forgiveness. Man must not expect more than those attributes which we offer to our God.

"Edmund Kean.

"Exchange Coffee-house."

The ill-success which attended this attempt at forgiveness will be fully explained by the following extracts, which we make from the Boston Papers:—

(From the Boston Daily Advertiser, Dec. 22.)

Theatre: Mr. Kean, last evening, attempted to make his appearance in the character of Richard, but, as we think might have been foreseen, was not permitted to play. The house was filled early, and the audience soon became quite noisy. At the hour for the curtain's rising, two of the managers and Mr. Kean successively attempted, two or three times, to address the house, but they were not permitted to be heard. Mr. Kean was severely pelted by missiles from the upper part of the house. A great tumult continued the whole time. Mr. Kilner came forward with a label, announcing that Mr. Kean declined playing, and with another, inquiring if the house would have the play go on without Mr. Kean. It was afterwards announced that Mr. Kean had left the house, and after some delay the curtain rose, and the play proceeded with Mr. Finn, in the part of Richard; but nothing was heard; and soon after the beginning of the Second Act, the play was stopped, and the curtain dropped. The noise then abated for a while, but the mob, who had assembled in great numbers in the street, began to rush into the house, and there being only two constables to oppose them, large sticks of wood were thrown into some of the boxes, and the work of dashing the chandeliers and tearing down the seats, boxes &c. immediately commenced. Everything in the theatre which could be destroyed was ruined, excepting the scenery, which was entirely untouched; the fragments from the boxes were thrown in heaps into the pit, and some apprehensions were entertained that the house would be set on fire, though no attempt of the kind was made.

(From the Boston Courier.)

Eight o'clock, Wednesday evening.—Kean has not been suffered to perform, nor even to speak to the audience at the theatre. He made two attempts, but was unsuccessful. A spontaneous and almost universal expression of disgust at his insolent and blasphemous letter, which he published in the morning, and of dissatisfaction with the course pursued by the Managers, was the forerunner to the decided and firm resolution manifested in the theatre, that he should not be permitted to appear on the stage. Mr. Finn attempted to play Richard, but at the end of the first act, the tumult was so great that the play was stopped. The crowd began to press upon the doors from the street, and at length forced a passage. The stairway leading to the second tier of boxes was so thronged, that it was impossible for those that were in to get out by that way, and many made their escape from the scene of confusion, by a window from the second storey, jumping about ten feet on to a shed, and from thence to the street. There is an immense throng in Franklin and Federal-street, which renders them, in the vicinity of the theatre, almost impassable.

The interior of the theatre, we understand, at this moment (half past nine), is almost entirely demolished, and the windows broken.—Mr. Justice Whitman read the Riot Act to the crowd outside, which, we believe, is still and peaceable. What is passing inside we know not. We beg leave to repeat a remark we made in our paper of this morning—*the Managers have assumed a fearful responsibility*.

Here is a chivalrous letter written in Kean's defence at the height of the storm.

MORNING POST, *January 31st, 1825*

"FOR THE DEFENDANT"

Sir,

For a number of years I have been a reader of your excellent Journal and have always observed it conducted with strict justice and impartiality. I do not wish to allude in any way to the unfortunate situation that Mr. Kean is now placed in with the public, but the following anecdote, the authenticity of which I can vouch for, I entreat you will give insertion to:—I was a summer at Brighton, when Mr. Trotter was manager of the theatre; one of his actors of the name of Conyngham, who had been a favourite performer in Dublin, Bath, &c. was engaged there, and like many of his tribe, was in great want of the *pecunia*. The prospect of getting a benefit was his only hope, but he was fearful of venturing to take one. A brother performer in the Brighton Company suggested the idea of writing to Kean who was then in the very zenith of his popularity at Drury Lane, to come and act for him. Poor Conyngham was afraid to make so bold a request, for though he had acted with him formerly at some provincial theatres, and always found him kind and affable to all his brother actors, yet Kean, a provincial actor, and the great Mr. Kean, the prop of Drury Lane theatre, might have changed his nature with his circumstances. However, he was induced to write to him, and by return of post, received the following answer. The letter I saw, and, to the best of my recollection, was as follows:—

"Dear Tom,—I this morning received your letter, and am sorry the world has not used you better. Put me for any part you please for next Thursday: I will, with all my heart, come and act for you. In the mean time, I beg you will accept the trifle I send you, to make the *pot boil*."

The enclosure was a 10*l*. bank note. True to his promise, he came (in a chaise and four) to the theatre and acted to a crowded audience; nor could he be induced to accept of one sixpence for his expenses. Such a trait deserves to be recorded as an instance of kindness and liberality shown to a worthy and a distressed man.

I am, Mr. Editor,

Your obedient servant,

VERITAS.

Covent Garden, Jan. 29.

THE STORM SUBSIDES

NEWS, *January 14th*, 1827

On Monday Mr. Kean, after divers troubles and turmoils by sea and land, somewhat suddenly appeared before a London audience:—not however as *Richard III*, the character with which he was wont invariably to commence his seasons, but as *Shylock*, the part in which he first sought metropolitan indulgence and renown. This was in some degree stepping forward as "a new man." The course was judicious: may he do more than "keep the promise to the ear." The house was crowded with friends, consequently his reception was tumultuously flattering. Of Mr. Kean's style of acting, our opinions are tolerably well known; therefore particular notice of *Shylock* will not be necessary. It did not strike us that he was improved; on the contrary we thought portions of the first scene especially, curiously indistinct; but his friends declare him to be unaltered and unalterable—therefore, we presume such must be the fact. After the performance, "Kean, Kean!" was boisterously called for: he complied with the request, bowed, and then with the best of eloquence, SILENCE, retired.

THE GREAT ELLISTON

"Look here, upon this picture and on this." Everybody knows Lamb's Essay beginning "Joyousest of once embodied spirits," and how at the end he dismisses the great Elliston with the words: "But, bless me, how *little* you look!" Drury Lane's manager was a man after Elia's own heart. "Did he *play* Ranger? and did Ranger fill the general bosom of the town with satisfaction? why should *he* not be Ranger, and diffuse the same cordial satisfaction among his private circles? with *his* temperament, *his* animal spirits, *his* good nature, *his* follies perchance, could he do better than identify himself with his impersonation? Are we to like a pleasant rake, or coxcomb, on the stage, and give ourselves airs of aversion for the identical character, presented to us in actual life?"

It is possible, nay, probable, that a less charitable portrait than Eia's would be nearer to the actual man. Some such view as that taken by Mr. Giles Playfair in his admirable work on Kean: "One cannot help feeling that the most colourful personality of the early nineteenth-century stage was born at least a hundred and fifty years too soon. How gloriously he would have served as the chief of a vast film organisation—sitting in a gaudy office surrounded by telephones and secretaries, thinking in millions and paying out thousands to script writers and actors, always being inaccessible—here, there and everywhere! And how he would have revelled in conferences with his publicity manager—contemplating magnificent new stunts, having his name written in huge letters across the sky! Yet he belonged very much to his own generation. He gambled and drank in a big way. (He did all things in a big way.) He was a poseur who loved to mystify his friends and subordinates, and to make long, flowery, absurdly exaggerated or untrue speeches. And he fascinated his contemporaries. Indeed, at the age of forty, he was an eminently successful man. With a salary of thirty pounds a week, he was the highest paid member of the Drury Lane Company and played both in tragedy and comedy, though better in comedy. He controlled two of London's minor theatres—the Surrey and the Olympic (which he had rechristened 'Little Drury')—and various other theatres in the provinces. He was the enthusiastic proprietor of a circulating library in Bristol which he called 'a literary association.' He hoped to stand for Parliament one day. And he yearned above everything to be given a knighthood. And after all, why not? He was well born, well educated, lived in a large house in Stratford Place (Mayfair) and knew everyone worth knowing from the Prince Regent downwards—or upwards."

Somewhere between the two views it is probable that we shall find the real Elliston. Possibly some light may be thrown on the subject by the following account of an action at law taken by one Mr. Poole, an author, against Elliston, who had kicked him. I give the account in full because it amuses me very much and I conceive that it may amuse others. Incidentally, it tells us a little more about The Book's collector, Mr. J. St. Aubyn, who now turns out to be Mr. James St. Aubyn, a barrister:

MORNING CHRONICLE, *June 2nd*, 1825

COURT OF KING'S BENCH—JUNE 1, 1825
(Middlesex Adjourned Sittings after Easter Term, before the Lord Chief Justice and Special Juries)

Poole v. *Elliston*. This was an action against Mr. Elliston of Drury Lane Theatre, for assaulting and kicking Mr. Poole, the author. Plea, Not Guilty.

Mr. Brougham (with whom was Mr. E. Alderson) stated the case. He said it had often been observed, that there was no species of cases, which varied from each other so much in character, as Actions of Assault. In some, the injury complained of was so slight, as to be unworthy the serious consideration of a Court of Justice; whilst, on the other hand, there were others, which required the serious animadversion of Juries, in the shape of exemplary damages. He must be permitted to say, that the present case appeared to him to be one of the latter description. The plaintiff was a person who bore the rank of a gentleman, and had acquired considerable reputation for his literary talents. From the year 1812 to 1820, he had occupied his leisure hours in writing for the Stage—an occupation in which many eminent men had employed themselves. He had written two Theatrical Pieces for Drury Lane Theatre, which had been very favourably received. It was the custom of the Theatre, when an author's work was successful in public estimation, to put his name on what is called the free list of the House; or, in other words, to give him a general passport to the Theatre, without paying any admission money. After the plaintiff's last Dramatic Work had been performed with success, he applied to the Defendant to have his name put on the free list, according to custom. The defendant, however, charged the plaintiff with having spoken of him in a way he did not approve. They had a conference upon the subject, and, in the result, Mr. E. thought it proper to withdraw Mr. P.'s name altogether from the free list. Several letters passed upon the subject, and at last the defendant was pleased to treat the plaintiff's correspondence with silent contempt. The defendant, it seemed, was a great person in Drury Lane Theatre, and probably from his situation at the head of that establishment, thought himself at liberty to show a higher bearing towards other persons than was usual in the private walks of society. This deportment the plaintiff thought was by no means justifiable, and therefore sought an opportunity of a personal interview, to require an explanation of the reason why his letters were treated with so much disrespect. There was nothing unusual or extraordinary in this. The Plaintiff called at Mr. Elliston's house on the 4th of December last for this purpose; he chose the morning, not wishing to disturb the plaintiff in his hours of relaxation and enjoyment; he knocked at the door, sent in his card, and was desired to walk upstairs. He had a friend with him, who also sent up his card, and they were both shown into a room. In a short time afterwards, Mr. Elliston entered the apartment in a violent rage, and storming with passion, he instantly addressed the plaintiff, in terms so gross and low, that he (Mr. Brougham) would spare himself the task of repeating them; he would not disgrace his lips with language so disgusting and coarse as Mr. Elliston thought proper to use; it was such as no man, whether gentleman or otherwise, would use towards another, or towards any person in his own situation of life. This was accompanied with a threat of personal violence if the plaintiff did not immediately leave the room, and in fact, before the plaintiff could obey the mandate, he began beating, and attempted to kick him. All this passed in the presence of the plaintiff's friend, who began to remonstrate with the defendant upon his outrageous conduct. In answer to something which the friend said, the defendant replied, "You are a liar, and I'll treat you in the same way;" and advised him not to provoke him with his observations, because he (Mr. E.) was a stronger man, and would do him a mischief. Mr. Elliston was a man certainly whose strength was undoubted, whatever opinion might be entertained of his mind and manners, either as an actor or as a gentleman. The plaintiff and his friend certainly did not wish to give him an opportunity of exercising his bruising powers, and therefore they hastily withdrew from the house. It could hardly be supposed, that Mr. Elliston was in a state of intoxication at that hour of the morning, even if he could plead inebriety as an excuse for such conduct. Had it been the evening, such a supposition would be still more improbable, because it was not to be imagined that as an actor, he could, in that state, do his duty in "holding the mirror up to nature" or perform his part "*veluti in speculum*," according to the motto of his theatre; for if such had been the case, it might with more propriety be said, that he was holding up an *ale-glass* instead of a *looking-glass* to his auditory (a laugh). Suffice it to say, that Mr. Elliston, though at an early hour of the morning, had used such language as would have disgraced a ticket porter, who, though he might not yield to Mr. Elliston in strength, would not compare with him in the correctness of language and manners. It was not to be expected therefore that Mr. Elliston would put his defence on the ground of drunkenness. The plaintiff did not complain in this action of bodily injury. He did not complain of the violence of a waggoner or a coal-heaver; but he complained of that which was tantamount to a fractured limb, considering that the outrage was committed upon him in the presence of his friend. He had sustained no bodily suffering, but he was insulted in a manner, which could not be endured in civilised society—he was kicked out of the house, and threatened with violence if he attempted to return. This was the nature of the case he had to lay before the Jury, and he hardly knew what damages would be too great for the defendant to pay. The plaintiff appealed to sensible men, with the feelings of gentlemen. It was the duty of the Jury to encourage men to appeal to the laws of their country—those laws alone, which ought to govern the conduct of civilised beings—and not by discouragement drive them to appeal to another description of laws, which hardly deserved the appellation of laws. When gentlemen were attacked in this way, they deserved commendation, for seeking redress in a Court of Justice. The Jury were representatives of the law as well as of the public, and in giving such damages as would encourage other plaintiffs to take this peaceful course, they would confer a benefit on society, and teach persons of the defendant's temper and disposition, to check their inclinations for outrage and violence.

Mr. James St. Aubyn, examined by Mr. Alderson: I am acquainted with the plaintiff; I accompanied him on the 4th of December last to Drury Lane Theatre; it was one o'clock at noon; we inquired for Mr. Elliston; I have the honour of being a barrister. After waiting a little time, the servant returned and desired us to walk upstairs; the plaintiff and myself had sent up our cards; we walked upstairs accordingly, and were shown into a room across the stage; shortly afterwards Mr. Elliston came into the room; he seemed, as I thought, in a very great passion, and said to the plaintiff, "Get out of this house or I'll kick your ——," using the grossest word (witness mentioned the word upon being desired by Counsel); Mr. Elliston "suited the action to the word" (a laugh), and did kick him in the part mentioned; the plaintiff remonstrated, and asked Mr. Elliston to hear him, and expressed a wish to speak; Mr. Elliston said he would hear nothing, and took hold of his collar to turn him out; I got between them, and said to Mr. Elliston, "If you won't hear Mr. Poole, at least hear me." Mr. Elliston said, "I won't hear anybody." Mr. Poole asked me what he was to do. I told him he had better leave the house as soon as possible. We immediately walked across the stage, and Mr. Elliston followed us. He said to Mr. Poole, "I don't strike you, because I should kill you." Mr. Elliston is a considerably larger man than Mr. Poole, who is a very little man. When Mr. Elliston said he would not strike Mr. Poole (for fear of killing him), I told him he had struck him. He turned sharp on me, and said, "You lie." I said, that was not language I had been used to. We walked downstairs as fast as we could and were followed by Mr. Elliston to the lobby, and he followed us into the street. He desired somebody at the door to turn us out, and never to let us in again. He insulted both of us. He told a person at the door to take notice of the plaintiff, and not admit him into the house in future.

Cross-examined by Mr. Scarlett: I have been fourteen or fifteen years at the bar. Immediately after we were turned out, I accompanied Mr. Poole before a Magistrate. He went before a Magistrate by my advice. I was not acquainted with Mr. Elliston. I sent my card up. Mr. Poole asked me to do it. Mr. Poole did not take me to the house as his counsel. Oh! dear, no! He did not consult me as counsel. I believe very few people do that (a laugh). I had nothing to say to Mr. Elliston. Mr. Poole requested me to send my card along with his. I had no other reason for sending it, except that Mr. Poole desired me. He wanted me to hear what Mr. Elliston said. He wanted me to be his witness; those were the very words he used, and I was ready to remain with him so long as Mr. Elliston conducted himself reasonably; I wished to mediate matters. (Mr. Scarlett produced a pamphlet and questioned the witness about it.) I am the person to whom that little book is dedicated. It is a little work written by Mr. Poole; I did not know from Mr. Poole whether he had or had not published any libels on Mr. Elliston; I am not aware of anything of that kind except that book; I am not aware of any altercation that had taken place between them. I had heard my friend Mr. Poole say that he had a misunderstanding with Mr. Elliston, but the particulars I was not aware of; I have heard the plaintiff say, that he had held Mr. Elliston up to public ridicule, but I don't remember his saying that he would do so again; I don't remember his saying that he had held him up to ridicule in the newspapers; I heard him say, that Mr. Elliston had refused his entering the Theatre on his claim of a free admission; I was to be the plaintiff's witness; that was the very expression which the plaintiff used; he asked me to be his witness; he had written a letter to the defendant, and having received no answer, he wished me to be a witness of what passed.

Upon my oath, he did not say that he was going to insult Mr. Elliston; we waited 20 or 25 minutes before we saw Mr. Elliston; it was the time of the rehearsal; I understood there was a rehearsal; we had to cross the stage; by my advice Mr. Poole went the same day before a Magistrate; Mr. E. appeared, and the plaintiff stated his case; I was not examined as a witness, but Mr. Poole mentioned to the Magistrate that I was a witness to what had taken place. I did not attend at the Sessions to support the indictment. I went out of town. Mr. Poole was bound over to prosecute. I did not advise him to change his plan, and bring an action instead of indicting the defendant for the assault. My advice was, to make a public example of him. I never thought that there was anything in the book alluded to which irritated Mr. Elliston. There was an interval of some months between the publication of the book and this assault. The book went out of my head entirely. If I had thought of the book, I don't know what I should have done when I was asked to accompany the plaintiff. Mr. Poole did not tell me he had published the offensive passages in the book in the newspapers. The moment Mr. Elliston saw the plaintiff, he appeared to be in a great passion. The kick was given immediately, and there was no time for running.

Mr. Hopwood, Clerk to the plaintiff's Attorney, proved that he had served notice upon the defendant, that the plaintiff did not mean to proceed with the prosecution for the assault. The defendant's recognizances were discharged by witness, at the plaintiff's expense. There was a letter written to the defendant to desire an apology, before the action was brought.

This was the plaintiff's case.

Mr. Scarlett then addressed the Jury for the defence. He agreed with his Learned Friend, Mr. Brougham, in the general observation, that there were no class of cases which admitted of so much variety in character, as actions of assault—that some were unworthy of serious consideration and that others required considerable damages at the hands of a Jury; but he differed from him in his conclusion, that this was a case of the latter description. There were some cases of this nature, which the imagination of Counsel might suggest as requiring the dignity of a special Jury and which demanded exemplary damages; but which, when the real facts came to be understood, produced a very different impression upon the minds of sober and sensible persons. The present was a case of that character. It was not an ordinary sketch of the imagination, to fancy a case where the complaining party had, by repeated insults, goaded the feelings of the supposed offender, until the provocation could no longer be endured, and after inviting that violence which it was not in human nature to restrain, then proceeded by indictment or action for the violence he had provoked. A case marked by such circumstances, he could hardly conceive required the consideration of a Special Jury, when the only point for deliberation must be, whether the damages should be a farthing or a shilling. It was admitted by the Plaintiff himself, that he had been holding up the defendant to public ridicule and contempt. He must, therefore, have been pretty well aware of the sort of reception he would have, when he obtruded himself upon the defendant. There had been a correspondence about the refusal of an admission to the Theatre. The plaintiff had known Mr. Elliston's determination upon the subject, and therefore the plaintiff had no right to expect an answer from him to his last letter. That Mr. Elliston was justified in refusing the admission no man could doubt, after the manner in which he had been confessedly ridiculed and libelled. It was a matter of discretion with the defendant, and he had a right to exercise that discretion. What then was the plaintiff's conduct? Having had his refusal, he took his friend to the defendant's house, obviously for no other purpose than to give fresh insult, and to invite that sort of violence of which he complained. Mr. St. Aubyn was no friend of Mr. Elliston, nor any visitor of his. Why then take an actual stranger? It was a very odd circumstance that Mr. St. Aubyn should send his card to a person with whom he had no communication to make. Was it not obvious that the plaintiff sought an interview under the cover of his friend's card, knowing that without some such device the defendant would have treated his own card with the contempt which the owner of it deserved? He (Mr. S.) did not mean to deny that the conduct of the defendant rendered him liable to a verdict. Far from it; but he entreated the Jury to consider the manner, and the circumstances under which the defendant had been betrayed into the act of violence. Any man under similar circumstances would have evinced the same intemperance. Men were not angels; they were subject to the infirmities of their common nature. It was conceded that the plaintiff must have a verdict; but the amount of damages was another question. Although his Learned Friend had told the Jury that the case deserved their serious consideration, yet he

(Mr. Scarlett) asked them whether, in their sober judgment they could give any more than nominal damages? If a man comes into a Court of Justice to ask for damages, he ought to satisfy the Jury that the wrong he complains of has not been brought upon him by himself; for if he invites personal inconvenience, courts the injury he receives, and solicits, by his own conduct, that which is inevitable, he has no right to demand serious damages. By the plaintiff's own admission, he had drawn upon himself those consequences of which he now complained. He had published a book in which he held the defendant up to ridicule and contempt, and then placed himself in a situation to provoke violence. He was, therefore, the author of his own wrong. Mr. St. Aubyn, whom he had not the pleasure of knowing, had candidly confessed, that if he had recollected the book which had been written by the plaintiff, perhaps he would have advised him not to visit the defendant. The advice which Mr. St. Aubyn gave him, to go before a Magistrate, and prosecute the defendant for the assault, was certainly most proper. By whom the plaintiff was desired to change the course of his proceeding afterwards, did not appear; but it was very artful advice, because, if the plaintiff had prosecuted by indictment, he must have been examined as a witness himself, and then he would have been obliged to tell the Jury the whole story; and the consequences would have been that the defendant would have been fined sixpence and discharged. But, by bringing an action, he exempted himself from the exposure which he must otherwise have made in the witness box, by confessing that he had insulted, libelled, and provoked the defendant to commit the act complained of. Enough, however, of the merits of the case was disclosed to justify the Jury in giving the plaintiff the verdict for the smallest current coin. The Jury would not exceed that amount without doing injustice to the defendant. They must not suppose that the plaintiff had a right to demand a free admission of Mr. Elliston. A prescriptive usage from the time of Thespis could not sanction that as a right, which was merely a matter of courtesy. If the plaintiff knew that the defendant had the misfortune to have an irritable temper, he had the less excuse for provoking that irritation. The defendant had no witnesses to call, because the only witness of the transaction was Mr. St. Aubyn; but with the admitted fact that the assault was committed under circumstances of great provocation, surely the Jury would have some regard for the feelings of human nature.

KEAN AS CORIOLANUS

KEAN AS OTHELLO

He submitted to their serious deliberation that, under all the circumstances, the case demanded no more than the most trifling damages.

The LORD CHIEF JUSTICE summed up the case, and observed, that although the plaintiff was entitled to a verdict, yet the Jury ought to take into consideration the circumstances under which the assault was provoked.

The Jury deliberated a few minutes, and found their verdict for the plaintiff—Damages, Eighty Pounds.

ST. AUBYN

Another version of the trial, which tells us more about St. Aubyn, who now appears as "Little St. Aubyn":

THE AGE, *June 5th*, 1825

The important trial of Poole versus Elliston (in spite of that silly old rogue the Chronicle saying on Monday that it had been settled to the *satisfaction* of both parties!) came on in the Court of King's Bench on Wednesday.

In case any of our readers should not be aware of the precise ground of complaint, we beg to tell them that last summer little Poole (as he is call'd) in a preface to a piece called *Married and Single*, issued a most violent and gross tirade against the great Elliston for breach of faith, in consequence of which his name was erased from the Drury Lane free list, and on Poole's calling with a friend at the Theatre to obtain an explanation, he got himself particularly well kick'd, and for the *past* action, brought the *present* one.

The Jury were apprized that, although Mr. Elliston was a man of great state *generally*, yet his *state* of an evening was sometimes such as to induce him to do some very funny things; but this, which was the funniest of all, was done in the morning, when he could not be supposed to be *in such good* spirits as at night—that, although, as a performer, his duty was "to hold the mirror up to nature," it did not follow that he was to *cast reflections* upon nature; and while he was bound "to show the very age and body of the time, his form and pressure," he was by no means bound to show "*his form and pressure*" to anybody else—that a blow on

H

any part of the person was bad enough; but when it went to *extremities*, it really was not to be borne—that, although he had removed little Poole from the "free list" of his Theatre, he had placed himself on it by "making more *free* than welcome," and that he should have been satisfied with striking him off in the one respect without *striking* him in any other respect—and, therefore, as Mr. Elliston having made a considerable hole in his own manners, as well as in the most delicate part of little Poole's honour, the *Kickee* had instituted proceedings against the *Kicker*, and in looking to the Jury for heavy damages, Brougham begged to inform them, that the length of Mr. Elliston's purse ought, in this instance, to be measured by the length of his foot.

Little St. Aubyn, who appeared as Poole's friend, and who, if standing on Poole's head, would make but a good-sized man, was examined, and stated that he went with him into Elliston's room, and on Elliston's appearance, he not only gave Poole to understand that he should kick—but he instantly adopted Hamlet's advice, and "suited the action to the word"—that the kick was so immediate, *there was no time for running!*— that when he told Elliston he *had* struck Poole, he gave him "the lie"—that though he had rather receive that than anything else from Mr. E., still it was unpleasant—that though a barrister, Poole did not consult him as counsel—*oh*, dear no—nobody did that,—and that on Poole's asking him what was best to be done, he told him the best thing was to get out of the house as quick as possible!! which it seems they both did; and, considering the state of the Lessee's irritation, it was decidedly the wisest plan to pursue. In spite, however, of a very smart speech from Scarlett, and a favourable charge from the Lord Chief Justice, the Jury (some of whom must evidently have been in Poole's situation) gave a verdict of 80*l.*; on hearing which, His Lordship shook his head, *though some thought there was nothing in it*. If Poole can get eighty pounds every time he gets kicked, we must say he is a fool to go on writing farces, for he will get more by the one than he can ever get by the other, as he can never write a better farce than the one acted at Westminster on this occasion; and his little honour having once gone through the operation with such éclat, it can matter little to him how often it is repeated.

We really think that Mr. Elliston, though very hasty, was provoked almost to a justification, and is therefore very ill-used by the Jury; but, as things have turned out, we recommend His

Majesty, the next time he makes up his mind "to put his foot in a *Pool*," to do it much more effectually than appears to have been the case on the present occasion.

ANECDOTE

And here is an ancedote about Elliston which might have made Lamb reconsider his "joyousest." It follows immediately on the law-case.

EXAMINER, *December 12th*, 1924

Last week was a busy one with a gentleman of high rank in the theatre, Drury Lane. His overthrow of a Dramatist in a fit of valour is already before the public—his attendance at the execution of Fauntleroy too (for, like the late George Selwyn, Mr. E . . . is an amateur in these matters) has been much talked of; but an occurrence at the Theatre on the same evening is not as well known as it deserves to be. During the performance an unhappy tabby cat very leisurely crossed the stage, and produced most mal-à-propos merriment. The cause was announced to the Manager. "Bring her before us," cried he. The feline delinquent was accordingly captured, and brought to the Manager by one of the attendants. "She is a fine one," said the fellow, rubbing down poor puss—"shall I turn her out, Sir?" Full of the subject of his morning's entertainment, the Monarch replied, "No—take her forth to the back yard; she shall be executed, and I myself will witness it." A number of performers were lamenting the calamity of poor Mrs. Bland when Mr. E . . . returned to the Green Room; Miss S . . . just then asked somebody, "Where is she?" "Dead," said the Manager. "Dead! when did she die?" "Within these three minutes." "How?" "She was hanged by the neck—I saw it done myself!"

NON-SHAKESPEARE

It must not be supposed that the great actors were always playing Shakespeare. There were a large number of other plays the taste for which it is difficult, if not impossible, for us to understand to-day. The most famous piece in the non-Shakespearian repertory is probably Thomas Otway's *Venice Preserved*. William Archer, writing in 1923, held that people are possibly alive to-day who have seen this play performed, not merely as an antiquarian curiosity, but as part of the living drama. One can only marvel that this piece of patent absurdity held the stage for so long. The fact remains that since its first performance in 1680 it has been revived *forty-seven* times as against *thirty-two* revivals of Shakespeare's *Henry V*. Otway's work has three great acting parts. Among the representatives of Jaffier and Pierre, two rôles of almost equal value, have been Betterton, Ryan, Quin, Garrick, Spranger Barry, Bensley, Pope, Henderson, John Philip Kemble, Charles Kemble, Cooke, Elliston, Kean, Macready and Phelps, all of whom were at any time quite ready to resign the one part and take a turn with the other. Among the Belvideras have been Mrs. Barry, Mrs. Cibber, Mrs. Siddons, Miss O'Neill, Mrs. Crawford, Fanny Kemble and Helen Faucit. In our own days Geneviève Ward played the distraught lady, and I have never ceased regretting having rashly missed that performance in 1920 by the Phœnix Society in which Ion Swinley, Baliol Holloway and our normally sensible Cathleen Nesbitt lent themselves to the turgid nonsense.

But let nonsense speak for itself. Jaffier, a young Venetian spendthrift, stands in the estimation of Priuli the senator very much as Bassanio stood to Antonio. The old man takes the young one into his house and makes much of him, and in return the young sorner steals his protector's daughter. The cash all gone, Jaffier comes crawling back and, appealing to his father-in-law, says:

> "There's not a wretch that lives on common charity
> But's happier than me. For I have known
> The luscious sweets of plenty; every night
> Have slept with soft content about my head,
> And never waked but to a joyful morning:
> Yet now must fall like a full ear of corn,
> Whose blossom 'scaped, yet's withered in the ripening."

But Priuli is not, as we vulgarly say, having any:

> "Home and be humble; study to retrench.
> Discharge the lazy vermin of thy hall,
> Those pageants of thy folly;
> Reduce the glittering trappings of thy wife

To humble weeds, fit for thy little estate.
Then to some suburb cottage both retire;
Drudge, to feed loathsome life; get brats, and starve—
Home, home, I say!"

To the discomfited Jaffier now enters Pierre, a disgruntled soldier who suggests to his bosom's friend that he should join in a conspiracy to unseat the Senate and dispose of the Senators by massacre. To put a particular edge on the general grievance, Peirre tells Jaffier that an execution of his domestic goods, the warrant being signed by Priuli, is in process at this very moment:

"Here stood a ruffian with a horrid face
   Lording it o'er a pile of massy plate,
   Tumbled into a heap for public sale.
   There was another making villainous jests
   At thy undoing. He had ta'en possession
   Of all thy ancient, most domestic ornaments,
   Rich hangings intermixed and wrought with gold;
   The very bed, which on thy wedding night
   Received thee to the arms of Belvidera,
   The scene of all thy joys, was violated
   By the coarse hands of filthy dungeon villains,
   And thrown amongst the common lumber."

Jaffier agrees to join the conspirators, who quite reasonably demand some sort of guarantee. Jaffier offers Belvidera as hostage, and handing over his dagger, says:

            "When I prove unworthy—
You know the rest—then strike it to her heart;
And tell her, he who three whole happy years
Lay in her arms and each night repeated
The passionate vows of still increasing love,
Sent that reward for all her truth and sufferings."

But Belvidera, misliking her company, decides to escape and does. She returns to Jaffier, and telling him that he is putting his money on the wrong horse, proposes that Jaffier should double-cross the conspirators by warning the Senate, including old Priuli, of the fate awaiting them:

> "Save the poor, tender lives
> Of all those little infants which the swords
> Of murtherers are whetting for this moment.
> Think thou already hears't their dying screams.
> Think that thou seest their sad, distracted mothers
> Kneeling before thy feet, and begging pity
> With torn, dishevelled hair and streaming eyes,
> Their naked, mangled breasts besmeared with blood,
> And even the milk with which their fondled babes
> Softly they hushed, dropping in anguish from 'em.
> Think thou seest this, and then consult thy heart."

To this Jaffier says, "Oh!" and Belvidera continues in this strain for some time. Ultimately Jaffier consents:

> "Come, lead me forward now like a tame lamb
> To sacrifice; thus in his fatal garlands,
> Decked fine and pleased, the wanton skips and plays,
>   Trots by the enticing, flattering priestess' side,
>   And much transported with his little pride,
>   Forgets his dear companions of the plain
>   Till by her, bound, he's on the altar lain;
>   Yet then too hardly bleats, such pleasure's in the pain."

This is the passage of which Archer says, "I think it would be hard to find, even in Restoration tragedy, a more undramatic speech, an image more inappropriate to the character and the situation." Now Jaffier's scheme to betray Pierre and his fellow conspirators comes to nothing, because Priuli has got wind of the plot on his own account, thus putting Jaffier in the ignominious position of the double-crosser who comes unstuck. Pierre is sentenced to be broken on the wheel, but is allowed a parting colloquy with Jaffier. And we must listen to the following:

> "JAFFIER. Speak aloud thy burthened soul,
>   And tell thy troubles to thy tortured friend.
> PIERRE. Friend! Couldst thou yet be a friend, a generous friend,
>   I might hope comfort from thy noble sorrows.
>   Heav'n knows I want a friend.
> JAFFIER.   And I a kind one,
>   That would not thus scorn my repenting virtue,
>   Or think, when he is to die, my thoughts are idle.

PIERRE. No! Live, I charge thee, Jaffier.
JAFFIER.   Yes, I will live,
   But it shall be to see thy fall revenged
   At such a rate as Venice long shall groan for.
PIERRE. Wilt thou?
JAFFIER. I will, by Heav'n!
PIERRE. Then still thou'rt noble,
   And I forgive thee. Oh—yet—shall I trust thee?
JAFFIER. No: I've been false already.
PIERRE.   Dost thou love me?
JAFFIER. Rip up my heart, and satisfy thy doubtings.
PIERRE (*He weeps*). Curse on this weakness!
JAFFIER. Tears! Amazement! Tears!
   I never saw thee melted thus before.
   And know there's something lab'ring in thy bosom
   That must have vent; though I'm a villain, tell me.
PIERRE (*Pointing to the wheel*). Seest thou that engine?
JAFFIER. Why?
PIERRE. Is't fit a soldier who has lived with honor,
   Fought nations' quarrels, and been crowned with conquest,
   Be exposed a common carcass on a wheel?
JAFFIER. Hah!
PIERRE. Speak! is't fitting?
JAFFIER. Fitting?
PIERRE. Yes, is't fitting?
JAFFIER. What's to be done?
PIERRE. I'd have thee undertake
   Something that's noble, to preserve my memory
   From the disgrace that's ready to attain it.
OFFICER. The day grows late, sir.
PIERRE. I'll make haste, O Jaffier,
   Though thou'st betrayed me, do me some way justice."

At this point Jaffier has the astounding:

   "No more of that. Thy wishes shall be satisfied.
   I have a wife, and she shall bleed; my child too
   Yield up his little throat, and all t'appease thee—"

About this Archer says: "No comment can do justice to the insane brutality of the mind which conceived this passage." But then Archer

was possibly blind to an aspect of the friendship between Jaffier
and Pierre which it is polite to call Renaissance. In the end Jaffier
stabs Pierre and then himself. In the meantime Belvidera has gone
mad. And to her in her madness the ghosts of Jaffier and Pierre
"rise together, both bloody." Belvidera is now due to expire:

"My husband bloody, and his friend, too!—Murther!
Who has done this? Speak to me, thou sad vision;
On these poor trembling knees I beg it. (*Ghosts sink.*)
                             Vanished—
Here they went down. Oh, I'll dig, dig the den up.
You shan't delude me thus.—Ho! Jaffier, Jaffier!
Peep up and give me but a look.—I have him!
I've got him, father: oh, now how I'll smuggle him!
My love! my dear! my blessing! help me, help me!
They have hold on me, and drag me to the bottom!
Nay—now they pull so hard—farewell—"

Johnson said of this nonsense: "The striking passages are in every
mouth; and the public seems to judge rightly of the faults and
excellences of this play—that it is the work of a man not attentive
to decency, nor zealous for virtue, but of one who conceived
forcibly, and drew originally, by consulting nature in his own
breast." To consider the opinions on this play held in the past by
highly educated and critical minds is an eye-rubbing process.
Roden Noel considered Belvidera "own sister to Cordelia, Imogen
and Desdemona." Walter Scott held that she had "rightly drawn
more tears than Juliet." Oddest of all, perhaps, are Hazlitt's reactions
to this piece. Writing in *The Times* in 1817, he says: "Otway's noble
tragedy of *Venice Preserved* was produced here last night. . . . Of Mr.
Johnstone's Pierre, after having seen Mr. Kemble in it, or even Mr.
Young, we cannot speak in terms of applause. The character is not
one of blunt energy, but of deep art. It is more sarcastic than fierce,
and even the fierceness is more calculated to wound others than to
shake or disturb himself. He is a master-mind, that plays with the
foibles and passions of others and wields their energies to his dangerous purposes with conscious careless indifference. Mr. Johnstone
was boisterous in his declamation, coarse in his irony, pompous
and common-place in his action. Mr. Rae (as Jaffier), in the famous
scene between the two characters, displayed some strong touches of
nature and pathos. Miss Campbell, as Belvidera, did not altogether

realise our idea of Otway's heroine; one of 'the most replenished sweet works of art or nature.' " The notice ends: "The play was given out for repetition with some marks of disapprobation from a part of the audience." And our own Professor Allardyce Nicoll holds that even Dryden never succeeded in producing "such a masterly work as *Venice Preserved.*" And hear Edmund Gosse on the play: "Out of the dead waste of the Restoration this one solitary work of supreme genius rose unexpected and unimitated." "Furthermore," says Gosse, "it is a noble and solid masterpiece . . . the poetic element is always severely subordinated to the dramatic. . . . All is designed for the true home of the drama, the stage; and without being in the least stagey, this theatrical aim is carried out with the most complete success. There are few plays in existence so original and so telling in construction as this." I will have nothing to do with all this laudatory nonsense. I hold with Archer that Otway's "masterpiece" is "based upon an ideal of drama which leaves wholly out of account any rational imitation of human actions or of human speech." And I read with a chuckle Byron's description of Belvidera as "that maudlin bitch of chaste lewdness and blubbering curiosity whom I utterly despise, abhor, and detest."

TALMA AGAIN

In the sixth and last volume of Mantzius's *History of Theatrical Art* occurs this passage:

"The laws and regulations which to this day govern the *Théâtre Français* are in all essentials the same as those prescribed by Napoleon, whether as First Consul or as Emperor. The elaborate fundamental law itself, which determines in the minutest detail the relations of the State to the National Theatre, the internal relations of the *sociétaires*, the numbers of pupils in training, the periods for débuts, the salaries of the teachers etc., was signed and issued by Napoleon during the fatal Russian campaign of 1812, at his headquarters amidst the burning ruins of Moscow, where he lay with the sorrowful remnants of the Grand Army—at one of the gloomiest and most arduous moments of his whole career, that is, when it might seem that he must have been fully occupied by quite other things than the internal arrangements of the *Théâtre Français* and the relations of the dramatic pupils to the

Conservatoire. These regulations, which have outlived more dynasties than one and survived more than one revolution, are still known as *le décret de Moscou*, and bear date: "Imperial Headquarters, Moscow, 15th October, 1812."

An actor after Napoleon's heart was Talma. François Joseph Talma bore the same relation to his predecessor Lekain that Edmund Kean bore to John Philip Kemble. He was a naturalistic actor endowed with exceptional emotional powers, and Napoleon loaded him with courtesies and money. The young artillery officer had been a friend of the rising young actor, and the Emperor was pleased to be the great actor's patron and coach! The rôle in which he coached him was Julius Cæsar in Corneille's *Pompée*. When Napoleon wanted to amuse his famous "parterre of kings," it was Talma he sent for. And now Talma dies. The date is October, 1826.

DEATH OF TALMA

OBSERVER, *October*, 1826

The following account of the last hours of this extraordinary man is given in a letter from Paris dated October 20th:—it was not until five o'clock yesterday morning that Talma began to be convinced, by the extreme prostration of all his faculties, and the film that spread itself before his eyes, that his dissolution was approaching. He could no longer distinguish the persons who surrounded him. He had two notaries called, in whose presence he confirmed the dispositions of his Will, which had been made three weeks before. After this exertion, his remaining strength scarcely sufficed to mutter, in an almost extinguished voice, the single word *adieu!* which he addressed to one of the notaries. Four hours after this, at thirty-five minutes past eleven o'clock, he breathed his last, apparently without any suffering. It is generally supposed that the malady which has proved fatal to him was an intestinal schirrus. M. Dupuytren was desirous of performing an operation, which he was convinced would have saved Talma, had he had strength enough to undergo it. This operation was to extract that portion of the intestines which, according to this celebrated surgeon, were twisted, and to replace them in their natural state. The opening of the body will show if M. Dupuytren's conjecture was correct. But convinced as he was of the efficacy of the operation, he was deterred from resorting to it by the state of extreme weakness to which Talma was reduced, in consequence of the total cessation of his digestive functions for 44 hours previous to his death. The singular fact of his having continued to live so long in such a state is attributed by the physicians to his remarkably strong constitution. One of these gentlemen has asserted that, on opening the body, the region of the breast and lungs will be found in the most healthy and intact state. One of the times the Archbishop of Paris (who has repeatedly endeavoured to gain admittance to Talma) presented himself at his house, and was refused by one of the patient's relations to be brought into his presence, he said, "You probably suppose my intentions are very different from what they are in reality. My motives are noble and elevated. For a long time back I have been endeavouring to procure from the Court of Rome, that the ridiculous excommunication pronounced against actors should be taken off, and the present circumstance may most powerfully conduct to the success of my endeavours. Talma dying in peace with the Church would furnish me with a puissant argument. Moreover, I promise you not to say a single word about religion until Talma shall himself mention the subject." It is said, that the last time the Archbishop called, and met, as before, with a refusal, he lost all patience, and vehemently apostrophised Talma's nephew, a physician, in the following terms: "Unfortunate man! See what a responsibility you are drawing on your head. Great as is my indignation, I cannot here punish you for such unworthy conduct—my religion forbids me. But on the Day of Judgment when all the souls of my flock shall appear in the presence of God, mine shall pursue yours and call upon it to answer for the loss of an immortal soul." The young physician listened calmly to these severe menaces, and firmly but respectfully refused to introduce his Grace. The Archbishop did not again return. Madame Vanhove, Talma's wife, also wished to be admitted to his bedside, but he refused to see her. She did not insist but said, "I am sorry not to be permitted to see him once more. Tell him, I entreat you, that I came to offer him to share my fortune with his children." Madame Vanhove has upwards of 40,000 fr. a year that had been left her by Dr. Moreau (De la Sarthe) with whom she had lived. It is precisely this fortune that prevented any reconciliation between her and Talma and induced him to refuse seeing her in his last moments. "As my wife is now wealthy," said he, "it would no doubt be said that I became reconciled to her through motives of interest. Her fortune places an insurmountable barrier between us." One of the theatrical journals of this morning gives the following account of Talma's last moment:—Talma preserved all his intellectual faculties to the last moment. He felt no acute pain, and only complained of having a cloud before his eyes. He perfectly recognised the friends around his bed, and on seeing Messrs. Jouy, Arnault and Dovilliers, he stretched out his arms, wept and embraced them. He said to his nephew, "The physicians know nothing of my disease. Recommend them to open my body, that it may be useful to my fellow-creatures"; and in a minute after he said, "*Let there be no Priests!* All I ask is not to be buried too soon." Some time before he exclaimed, "What do they require of me—to make me abjure the art to which I owe all my glory, an art that I idolise? to deny the forty brightest years of my life? to separate my cause from that of my comrades, and to acknowledge them to be infamous? Never!" A few moments before his death, he murmured in a faint voice, "Voltaire! Voltaire! Voltaire!" Thus the greatest tragedian of his age expired in invoking the name of the greatest tragic genius of the last age.

The French papers of Saturday contain the following account of the opening of the body:—

"The body of Talma was opened this day at noon, by Dr. Breschet, in presence of the physicians and surgeons who attended on him during his fatal illness. It was discovered, from inspection, that what had been advanced several months ago, was perfectly correct—namely that the cause of this celebrated actor's death was a complete obliteration for nearly two inches in length, of the large intestine, at about six inches from its termination. In the other parts of the bowels there was a secondary inflammation observable. It is obvious that the obliteration above noticed must have rendered vain all the cares of the first medical men of the capital. There was also found an aneurismal tumour at the point of the heart, the existence of which had not been suspected during his life-time."

His nephew, almost immediately after his death, sent the following letter to the Paris Journals, and it seems well calculated to defeat those outrages against humanity which the Clergy of

France have sometimes displayed towards deceased actors and actresses:—

"To the Editor of the Etoile.

"Sir—Talma died this morning at 35 minutes past 11 o'clock. He has repeatedly, and in the presence of many of his friends, expressed a wish to be carried directly from his own house to the place of his last rest.

"I beg, Sir, you will have the goodness agreeably to the last wish of my uncle, to give all possible publicity to this declaration.

"(Signed) AMÉDÉE TALMA, M.D.

"Paris, Oct. 19."

Agreeably to his latest wish, the mortal remains of Talma were carried, on Saturday, directly from his house to the cemetery of Père-la-Chaise. Precisely at ten o'clock the funeral procession commenced its movement. It consisted of a rich hearse, drawn by four horses, fifteen mourning coaches, Talma's own carriage, the carriages of Mesdemoiselles Mars and Duchesnois, and several other carriages, nobody being in them, and the blinds being down. In an open carriage was Madame Rousta (Mademoiselle Volnais) in mourning, and immediately after her M. Ancelot and M. Soumet; and finally, in a third carriage, M. Casimir Perrier and his two sons. In the first mourning carriage we distinguished M. Arnault, the father, and M. Jouy, clothed in the costume of the Institute. All the other carriages were empty, the fineness of the weather having permitted Talma's friends, who were to have occupied them, to follow the procession on foot, which they preferred. The number of persons assembled amounted to between three and four thousand, most of them young men, and at their head were some persons distinguished by decorations of honour. M. Méchin was in his costume of Deputy, and all the Performers of the Royal Theatres proceeded bareheaded, and in the greatest order, preserving the most profound and respectful silence; a great number displayed in their countenances the excessive sorrow they experienced. The procession reached the cemetery about half-past eleven o'clock. The place of interment was on one of the heights to the right, not far from the monument of Marshal Masséna, and close to that of the family of Despaux. At the middle of the difficult ascent which leads to it, the hearse stopped. Twelve young men then took the coffin, and carried it in their arms to the brink of the grave destined to receive it. From the early part of the morning a crowd amounting, perhaps, to twenty thousand persons, had filled the cemetery, and at the moment when the procession arrived, they all collected round the grave. It was with difficulty that the coffin was carried to the grave, and that the friends and the orators were able to reach the same spot. With the exception of this trifling inconvenience, which was only the consequence of an excusable eagerness, everything was conducted with the utmost decorum.

The best description of Talma's acting is to be found in Macready's *Diary*:

The genius of Talma rose above all the conventionality of schools. Every turn and movement as he trod the stage might have given a model for the sculptor's art, and yet all was effected with such apparent absence of preparation as made him seem utterly unconscious of the dignified and graceful attitudes he presented. His voice was flexible and powerful, and his delivery articulate to the finest point without a trace of pedantry. There was an ease and freedom, whether in familiar colloquy, in lofty declamation, or burst of passion, that gave an air of unpremeditation to every sentence, one of the highest achievements of the histrionic art. It is a custom with many actors purposely to reach their dressing-rooms in just sufficient time to go on the stage, in order to avoid the nervousness which waiting for their entrance occasions. But Talma would dress some time before, and make the peculiarities of his costume familiar to him; at the same time that he thereby possessed himself more with the feeling of the character. I thought the practice so good that I frequently adopted it, and derived great benefit from it. His object was not to dazzle or surprise by isolated effects: the character was his aim; he put on the man, and was attentive to every minutest trait that might distinguish him. To my judgment he was the most finished artist of his time, not below Kean in his most energetic displays, and far above him in the refinement of his taste and extent of his research, equalling Kemble in dignity, unfettered by his stiffness and formality.

There is a curious thing to be noted about Macready; which is that he contrived to be at one and the same time lofty of soul and mean of mind. Consumed with envy of his betters, he yet had the sense to recognise them. "That low man" he called Kean; but at the moment of vituperation he was saying under his breath, "that magnificent actor."

ROYAL PATRONAGE

The King visits Covent Garden Theatre

Morning Herald, *December 1st*, 1826

The King, agreeably to previous announcement, honoured this theatre by his presence last night; and, as usual, on such occasions, its treasury had substantial reason to know that "the King's name is a tower of strength." For hours before the commencement of the performances, every door—from the portico even to the one-shilling gallery—was beset by crowds of strugglers for admission; though every *take-able* seat in the house had been taken before the close of the preceding day. Consequently, John Bull had a glorious opportunity of displaying his gallantry, by sticking his elbows against the fair necks of his half-fainting country-women, and making them shriek aloud, to the great edification of every foreigner present. "Every one for himself and God for us all!" is John's motto wherever there is a sight to be seen; and with his own money in his own fist, he elbows his way through all impediments without care of the consequences. "Oh! for pity's sake, sir? take your elbow from my face!" said a delicate little lady at the box entrance, to a portly powdered personage, who was working his well-dressed corpus forward inch by inch, by placing his elbow against her cheek. "Don't tell me, Ma'am!" said he—turning his sweaty scarlet visage upon her— "I'm not going to lose my chance of getting in; and if you can't bear a little crushing, you have no business here!" The poor lady had nobody with her but a slender youth, and of course he could effect nothing against so much brawn; but, luckily for her, somebody put an elbow against her oppressor's paunch with such vigour that he was constrained to give back a little, and thereby the lady was released from her painful predicament. This is but one instance out of hundreds; for shrieks and gruntings and imprecations were to be heard at every door; and so they always will be whilst John Bull remains as he is. Heaven mend him!

The King came from St. James's Palace, by way of Charing

Cross, St. Martin's Lane, Long Acre, James-Street and Hart-Street to the Royal entrance in Prince's Place—and a more unroyal approach than Hart-Street cannot well be imagined—a dirty, narrow, ill-paved and ill-lighted passage; lined with ruinous stables, little barbers' shops and houses of ill-fame. His Majesty's carriage was preceded by five other Royal carriages filled with the Officers of the Household, and other attendants; the servants all in full state liveries, and the cavalcade escorted by a party of the Life Guards. The four first carriages drove past Princes Place, towards Bow Street, and set down by the side of the theatre; from whence the courtiers they contained had to scamper back on foot through the mud, and crowds of squabblers, to Princes Place. In the meantime the King and his more immediate attendants—among whom we observed the Dukes of Wellington, Dorset and Montrose—had alighted at the Royal entrance to the theatre in Princes Place,—and a flourish of trumpets announced his arrival.

The King wore a military full dress of blue and gold, with the blue riband and a profusion of glittering orders. He entered the State box prepared for his reception, a few minutes before seven o'clock, surrounded by the Noblemen above-mentioned, and others of his attendants. The audience rose instantly, *en masse*, and received him with loud huzzas and waving of hats and handkerchiefs so long continued that his Majesty must have been almost wearied with bowing his acknowledgments of the tumultuous welcome. "God Save the King," followed by "Rule Britannia" was then sung by the performers, the audience all standing, and joining heartily, though a little discordantly in the choruses. His Majesty also remained standing throughout both the songs, and occasionally joining in the chorus.

The performances chosen by his Majesty were *Oberon* and *The Scapegoat*; and he seemed much amused, frequently applauding the exquisite singing of Miss Paton, Madame Vestris, and Sapio; and laughing heartily at the whimsical distresses of Farren in the afterpiece. At the close of the play, "God Save the King" and "Rule Britannia" were again called for by the audience; and they were sung by the performers, the King and the audience standing and joining in the chorus as before; and again at the conclusion of the performances "God Save the King" was repeated for the fourth time, as heartily as at first. His Majesty then bowed distinctly to every part of the house, and immediately withdrew,

KEAN AS IAGO

KEAN AS RICHARD III

amidst loud cheerings, which were repeated by the assembled multitude outside the theatre, as he entered his carriage to return to the Palace.

And Drury Lane

Morning Herald, *December 2nd*, 1826

Last night, this theatre was, in its turn, honoured and enriched by the presence of the King. Rumour had been very busy all day endeavouring to make people believe that Old Drury's new Manager meant to "do the thing more genteelly" than his rivals at "the Garden"—that, though a foreigner and a Republican, he would teach John Bull the respect due to Royalty and would not make a show of England's King for the sake of filthy lucre; that, in a word, he would not admit one single person more than could find "comfortable sitting room." But Rumour was wrong; for more people were admitted than could find comfortable standing room; or any standing room at all indeed—except in the lobbies and saloons among the "unfortunate girls." Everything, as far as we could observe, was conducted upon the same money-making plan as at the other house—the same demolition of shawls and head-dresses at the entrances; the same kicking at the box doors by payers who could not get a peep; the same re-demanding of money from the bother'd box-keepers; the same replying "Can't help it, sir—every place was engaged two days ago"— the same bringing out of dishevelled and fainting ladies to be resuscitated in the lobbies; the same squabbling between the takers of places about places taken; the same threats of turning out for standing up where there was no room to sit down; the same waiting for turns at every little peep-hole in the box doors —ten pairs of anxious eyes to each; the same bubble, bubble, toil and trouble, pains, puffing and perspiration, here and there, and everywhere; and pretty nearly the same amount of the root of all evil transferred from the pockets of the public to the treasury of the establishment. So that rogue Rumour was entirely wrong— but what then? The presence of a King cannot be had every night and "make hay while the sun shines," is a very respectable old proverb!

The King arrived in the same state as on the preceding evening at the other house; and he entered his box punctually at seven o'clock; thereby setting a very wholesome example to those of

I

his liege subjects who endeavour to distinguish themselves from the vulgar, by coming in *last* to the cry of *"first* company"!

The moment his Majesty appeared the audience rose, uncovered, and greeted him with loud and long-continued shouts of welcome which he very graciously acknowledged by bowing on every side. The National Anthem was sung by the performers; and though his Majesty remained standing the whole time, the audience would have it sung again—for John Bull likes to have his pennyworth for a penny; and seeing his King but seldom, he prudently makes the most of him when he does happen to get into his company.

The opera of the *Devil's Bridge* and the farce of *Love, Law and Physic*, were the performances chosen for the evening by his Majesty; and strange as it may appear, his Majesty never once turned his back upon the stage whilst the performers were on it, nor interrupted its business by talking aloud to the Noblemen around him; which certainly was very unfashionable—or at least, it was very contrary to the practice, as by supposed fashionables established; and really many of the Ladies seemed to be hardly able to know what to make of it. Nevertheless they kept their temper; everything passed off joyously; Corn-questions and Catholics were totally forgotten; Braham was in fine voice, and was applauded to the very echo. Liston and Harley excited lots of laughter—in some of which his Majesty did not disdain to join very heartily. "God Save the King" and "Rule Britannia" were sung and sung again in obedience to the clamorous call of the house; and finally, his Majesty retired amidst universal cheering, both within and without the walls thereof.

THE CONTEMPORARY DRAMA

"Who remembers a single thing that Lamb, or Hazlitt, or Leigh Hunt, or John Forster, or George Henry Lewes, ever said of a contemporary play?" Now, not even William Archer can have it both ways. The answer to him is Lewis Carroll's

> "You could not see a cloud, because
> No cloud was in the sky;
> No birds were flying overhead—
> There were no birds to fly."

And Archer has admitted that there was no contemporary drama in the time of Hazlitt. To be accurate, there was one dramatist who comes within The Book's praise. This was Sheridan Knowles, about whose *Virginius* Archer wrote: "Knowles was doubtless an early product of the pseudo-Elizabethanism fostered by Lamb's *Specimens*. But he was not misled into taking Webster and Ford for his models. His Elizabethan inspiration he drew, in the main, from Massinger; but his verbosity and his commonness derived rather from the Restoration. I am old enough to remember the time when he was taken seriously as a dramatist. I have seen several of his plays presented, not as curiosities, but as living masterpieces, making a direct appeal to the sympathies and the pockets of playgoers. I know of few men who have made any considerable success on the stage with less genuine talent to account for it. His art lay wholly in stodgy rhetoric, less bombastic, indeed, than that of Lee and Otway, but all the more flat and tedious". I have never seen a play by Knowles, but I mistrust him. To read, Knowles's plays are an extraordinary mixture of rodomontade and bathos. To account for their success Archer assumes that Knowles possessed some trick of the scene, or perhaps some energy of rhetoric. But I have never been able to divine the secret of his acceptance. He had not even the flashy theatricalism of Bulwer Lytton.

The first performance of *Virginius* took place on May 17th, 1820. Macready, who played the title rôle, says: "The early scenes were not unattended with danger, Charles Kemble being so hoarse that not one word, spoken in the lowest whisper, could be heard; but the action of the scene told its story with sufficient distinctness to keep alive its interest. This grew as the play advanced, and in the third act, in Icilius's great scene, Kemble's voice came out in all its natural strength, and brought down thunders of applause. With the progress of the play the rapt attention of the audience gradually kindled into enthusiasm. Long-continued cheers followed the close of each succeeding act; half-stifled screams and involuntary ejaculations burst forth when the fatal blow was struck to the daughter's heart; and the curtain fell amidst the most deafening applause of a highly-excited auditory. The play was an unquestionable triumph, which Knowles had sat in the pit to witness and enjoy." *The Times* said the next day:

Macready deserves peculiar praise for his Virginius. His acting is always excellent; but he has in this character touched the passions with a more masterly hand, and evinced deeper pathos than we recollect on any former occasion. The tone with which in the judgment scene he uttered the words—"My poor child here, who clings to me for protection"—was truly pathetic. Some embarrassment arose from the entangling of a knife in the folds of his robe, which injured the general effect; but the blow when given was terrific. As a catastrophe nothing could be finer, and the play should end, if possible, as that of Alfieri does, with the line from Livy, addressed to Appius, "With this blood I devote thy head to the infernal Gods."

In July of the same year we find Hazlitt writing:

Virginius is a good play:—we repeat it. It is real tragedy; a sound historical painting. Mr. Knowles has taken the facts as he found them, and expressed the feelings that would naturally arise out of the occasion. Strange to say, in this age of poetical egotism, the author, in writing his play, has been thinking of Virginius and his Daughter, more than of himself! This is the true imagination, to put yourself in the place of others, and to feel and speak for them. Our unpretending poet travels along the high road of nature and the human heart; and does not turn aside to pluck pastoral flowers in primrose lanes, or hunt gilded butterflies over enamelled meads, breathless and exhausted,—nor does he, with vain ambition, "Strike his lofty head against the stars." So far, indeed, he may thank the Gods for not having made him poetical. Some cold, formal, affected, and interested critics have not known what to make of this. It was not what they would have done. One finds fault with the style as poor, because it is not inflated. Another can see nothing in it, because it is not interlarded with modern metaphysical theories, unknown to the ancients. A third declares that it is all borrowed from Shakespeare, because it is true to nature. A fourth pronounces it a superior kind of melodrama, because it pleases the public. The last two things to which the dull and envious ever think of attributing the success of any work (and yet the only ones to which genuine success is attributable), are Genius and Nature. The one they hate, and of the other they are ignorant. We have described this class of critics more than once, but they breed still: all that we can do is to sweep them from our path as often as we meet with them, and to remove their dirt and cobwebs as fast as they proceed from the same noisome source.

There is a great deal more in this strain. Is it not possible that Hazlitt would not have liked this play so much had he not hated his fellow-critics more? The notice ends by describing *Virginius* as Macready's best and most faultless performance. And then there is a nice sentence about Miss Foote beginning " 'the freeborn Roman maid,' with a little bit, a delightful little bit, of the English school-girl in her acting." Of how many English actresses has not one wanted to say this?

DEARTH OF ACTRESSES

What of the actresses who held the stage between the retirement of the Siddons in 1812 and the appearance in 1829 of her niece Fanny Kemble? Here, perhaps, is the place for a few words about that young lady whom, to-day, we should vulgarly dismiss as a dear and a dud. Just as Macready was the stage's first gentleman, so Fanny was its first lady. Like Macready, she despised her profession, but unlike him she couldn't act. "Does not know the first rudiments of her art," wrote "the great W. C. M." But then Fanny was a blue-stocking who composed plays. And Fanny had sent her first play to Mr. Macready, who, while turning it down, found it "most painful, almost shocking, but full of power, poetry and pathos." And the entry in the Diary ends: "She is one of the most remarkable women of the present day." And one of the worst actresses, he added mentally. Fanny had become a Mrs. Butler, and here are the entries for the dates on which Fanny made her first appearances as Macready's leading lady. The year is 1848:

London, February 21st.—At Princess's Theatre, Macbeth. Mrs. Butler as Lady Macbeth.
February 23rd.—Wolsey. Mrs. Butler as Queen Katharine.
February 25th.—Othello. Mrs. Butler as Desdemona.
March 3rd.—Birthday, *aet.* fifty-five. Acted King Lear in my best manner, which was appreciated by the audience. Called for, led on by Mrs. Butler, warmly received.

After which he does not mention the lady again! And now peruse Fanny's account of the same week:

I act Lady Macbeth on Monday, on Wednesday Queen Kath-arine, and on Friday Desdemona, for the first time in my life. I have a beautiful and correct dress for her (you know I always liked my clothes), for which, nevertheless, I expect to be much exclaimed against, as our actresses have always thought proper to dress her in white satin. I have arrayed her in black (the only habit of the noble Venetian ladies) and gold, in a dress that looks like one of Titian's pictures.

That smothering scene, my dear Harriet, is most extremely horrible . . . I think I shall make a desperate fight of it, for I feel horribly at the idea of being murdered in my bed. The Desde-monas that I have seen, on the English stage, have always appeared to me to acquiesce with wonderful equanimity in their assasination. On the Italian stage they run for their lives round their bedroom, Pasta (*sic*) in the opera (and Salvini in the tragedy, I believe), clutching them finally by the hair of the head, and then murdering them. The bedgown in which I have arrayed Desdemona for the night would hardly have admitted of this flight round the stage; besides that, Shakespeare's text gives no hint of any such attempted escape on poor Desdemona's part; but I did think I should not like to be murdered, and therefore, at the last, got up on my knees on the bed, and threw my arms tight round Othello's neck (having previously warned Mr. Macready, and begged his pardon for the liberty), that being my notion of the poor creature's last appeal for mercy.

Readers will remember that the time came when Macready decided to do his smothering of Desdemona out of sight. And quite right too! As well a mill-stone round a leading man's neck as a leading lady. I visualise Fanny as an intense little thing. She meets Carl Maria von Weber, and her biographer writes: "Fanny did not forget *Oberon*. She could sing it, and often did, in the semi-privacy of her woodland walks—from beginning to end." And I am convinced she was always an amateur. She makes her first appearance as Juliet, which part she plays one hundred and twenty nights "sometimes beautifully, sometimes fairly, sometimes utterly badly." In other words, like an amateur. Now she tackles Belvidera, and Harness writes that "It is exactly like looking at Mrs. Siddons through the wrong end of an opera-glass." We read, too, of her being so moved by the emotions of Otway's heroine that she ran screaming down the stairs and would have fled into the street if her father had not followed and carried her back. But an obedient little girl, ready to play Juliet to her parent's Romeo, Belvidera to his

Jaffier, and, in Murphy's *Grecian Daughter*, to find all her performances bound each to each by filial piety. During the run of *Romeo
and Juliet* Fanny is introduced to Felix Mendelssohn-Bartholdy and
then begins a rain of presentations to the great Sir Walter Scott, the
railroad-minded Mr. Stephenson, Mr. Tennyson, King William and
Queen Adelaide, the Russells, the Hollands, the Grevilles. And so
Fanny continues acting when she must, and moving in good society
when she can, until the time comes when people are presented to
her—Mr. Dickens, Mr. Carlyle, Mr. Longfellow, Mr. Monckton
Milnes, Mr. Browning. All of whom, I must think, could not turn
poor Fanny into an actress, though it seems that her readings from
Shakespeare were admirable. In other words she was the spiritual
progenitor of Mary Anderson. We are concerned, here, however,
with Fanny's beginnings, and here is *The Times* on the subject:

> Upon the whole, we do not remember to have ever seen a more
> triumphant début. That Miss Kemble has been well and carefully
> instructed, as, of course, she would be, is clear; but it is no less
> clear that she possesses qualifications which instruction could not
> create, although it can bring them to perfection. We shall have
> probably many further opportunities of returning to the subject,
> and unless that should happen in this case which never yet did in
> any other, that an actress whose first essay has been so excellent
> shall prove less on future occasions, it may be reasonably expected
> that Miss Kemble will prove a great acquisition to the dramatic
> strength of the theatre.

What actresses are there between the withdrawal of the Aunt in
1812 and the arrival of the Niece in 1829? Well, there is Mrs. Dobbs
who "made such a pretty, insipid little rustic of Lady Teazle, show-
ing her little teeth like the painted dolls in a peruke-maker's window." There is Mrs. Alsop, a daughter of Mrs. Jordan, of whom
Hazlitt writes:

> A Lady of the name of Alsop, a daughter of Mrs. Jordan (by
> a former husband) has appeared at Covent-Garden Theatre, in
> the character of Rosalind. Not only the circumstance of her rela-
> tionship to that excellent actress, but the accounts in the papers,
> raised our curiosity and expectations very high. We were unwill-
> ingly disappointed. The truth is, Mrs. Alsop is a very nice little
> woman, who acts her part very sensibly and cleverly, and with a
> certain degree of arch humour, but "no more like her mother

than we to Hercules." When we say this, we mean no disparage-
ment to this lady's talents, who is a real acquisition to the stage in
correct and chaste acting, but simply to prevent comparisons,
which can only end in disappointment. Mrs. Alsop would make a
better Celia than Rosalind. Mrs. Jordan's excellences were all
natural to her. She was all gaiety, openness, and good-nature. She
rioted in her fine animal spirits, and gave more pleasure than any
other actress, because she had the greatest spirit of enjoyment in
herself. Her Nell—but we will not tantalise ourselves or our
readers. Mrs. Alsop has nothing luxurious about her, and Mrs.
Jordan was nothing else. Her voice is clear and articulate, but
not rich or flowing. In person she is small, and her face is not pre-
possessing. Her delivery of the speeches was correct and excellent as far as it went, but without much richness or power. Lively
good sense is what she really possesses.

After which exit Mrs. Alsop. And there is "that little pouting
slut, Miss Stephens, too greatly adored of Irish and Scotch audiences
to give much time to the English." We are, then, thrown back upon
the actress who is always called Miss O'Neill.
I think I have read every word that Hazlitt wrote about her, and
here are one or two passages marked by the most obvious sincerity:

Miss O'Neill's Isabella, though full of merit, disappointed us;
as indeed she has frequently done of late. Her "Oh fie, fie," was
the most spirited thing in her performance. She did not seize with
much force the spirit of her author, but she seemed in complete
possession of a certain conventicle twang. She whined and sang
out her part in that querulous tone that has become unpleasant
to us by ceaseless repetition. She at present plays all her parts in
the Magdalen style. We half begin to suspect that she represents
the bodies, not the souls of the women, and that her forte is in
tears, sighs, sobs, shrieks and hysterics. She does not play either
Juliet or Isabella finely. She must stick to the commonplace
characters of Otway, Moore, and Miss Hannah More, or she will
ruin herself.

And:

Miss O'Neill's Lady Teazle at Covent Garden Theatre appears
to us to be a complete failure. It was not comic; it was not elegant;
it was not easy; it was not dignified; it was not playful; it was not

anything that it ought to be. All that can be said of it is, that it was not tragedy. It seemed as if all the force and pathos which she displays in interesting situations had left her, but that not one spark of gaiety, one genuine expression of delight, had come in their stead. It was a piece of laboured heavy still-life. The only thing that had an air of fashion about her was the feather in her hat. It was not merely that she did not succeed as Miss O'Neill; it would have been a falling-off in the most commonplace actress who had ever done anything tolerably. There was a perpetual affectation of the wit and fine lady, with an evident consciousness of effort, a desire to please without any sense of pleasure. There was throughout an equal want of delicacy and spirit, of ease and effect, of nature and art. It was in general flat and insipid, and where any thing more was attempted, it was overcharged and unpleasant.

Nevertheless, Hazlitt could say on the occasion of this actress's marriage:

Next to Mr. Kean, the greatest tragic performer now on the stage is undoubtedly Miss O'Neill. She cannot take rank by the side of her great predecessor, but neither can any other actress be compared with her. If we had not seen Mrs. Siddons, we should not certainly have been able to conceive any thing finer than some of her characters, such as Belvidera, Isabella in *The Fatal Marriage*, Mrs. Beverley, and Mrs. Haller, which (as she first played them) in tenderness of susceptibility, and the simple force of passion, could not be surpassed. She has, however, of late, carried the expression of mental agony and distress to a degree of physical horror that is painful to behold, and which is particularly repulsive in a person of her delicacy of frame and truly feminine appearance.

In plain English, if Mrs. Siddons is the standard, Miss O'Neill was a second-rater.

CRAZY NIGHTS

What of the theatre's lighter side? Can our grandfathers and great-grandfathers have been wholly serious? Were there no spectacles? Here are two:

COVENT GARDEN

THE NEWS, *April 12th*, 1824 [? Author]

By some extraordinary coincidence, there is such a remarkable similarity between the Easter Romances at the two National Theatres, that, having seen the one at this house first—when we went to the other theatre, we declared that Drury Lane had copied Covent Garden! Which is the original, and which the *second* original, we shall not undertake to say; and be the fact as it may, it is satisfactory to be able to state that each posssesses great scenic merits.

The *Egyptian* romantic tale of enchantment, brought out on Monday last at Covent Garden, is called The Spirits of the Moon. The story alludes to the good genius and the evil genius, and the consequences of obeying them. Zerack, (Mr. Farley) obeys the bad principal. He usurps the throne of Egypt; he removes the rightful heir, Amasis (Miss Love) by means of his confidant, Norad (Mr. T. P. Cooke); and he seeks by forcible means to possess himself of the hand of the Princess Zephina (Miss Beaumont), the niece of the late King. But the confidant, as usual, is the Marplot of these wicked schemes.

Amasis, under the assumed name of Mirza, is summoned from the Arab's tent, where he had remained in seclusion, by the virtuous guardian of his fate; and after divers difficulties, by his aid, he descends into the lower regions and wrests from the hands of the base power which Zerack serves, the gifted bow and arrow that guards the race of the young prince. Zerack powerfully, but vainly, resists; the Fates and Norad are against him, and of course, the young prince Amasis, or Mirza, obtains the Throne of his ancestors. Miss Love was the young Prince, and played the character interestingly, but somewhat too bashfully; she appeared to be ill at ease in her partially masculine attire. She had a song entitled "Sweet Hope"—but the burden of it was "Sweet Home"; and though it was not an air that extorted applause by its imposing splendour, it afforded Miss Love an excellent opportunity of displaying the peculiar and deep tones of her voice. Mr. Farley is becoming rather an "overgrown" tyrant, but he sustained the character with all his wonted legitimate sternness of front— Mr. T. P. Cooke, as usual, dressed and looked the Egyptian attendant uncommonly well. There were some other parts to relieve the solemnity of the scene; such as Steelpinstitch, a wine-loving tailor; Benricup, a loquacious face-making overseer to the usurper; and Marmazetta, a slave, full of antics;—and those characters were severally most efficiently personated by Mr. Blanchard, Mr. Meadows, and Mr. J. S. (or young) Grimaldi.

There were some good scenes—but the first, the reflux of the Nile, by no means equalled our expectations. Zerack's secret chamber, with the sun-rays thrown into it, and the shade of Norad's person as he passed along behind the gloomy usurper, were well managed, but the great scenic effort of the evening was that with the proportionably long name—a *Polemporeremoporokinetikon*!! It represented a caravan of various Merchants on their Halt, after crossing the Desert and terminating with their arrival at the Antient Mart of the great City. This moving scene afforded various excellent specimens of the ancient ruins and remains of Egypt, and an impressive idea of the burning dreariness that those indefatigable Merchants and Agents have to surmount who cross those memorable Deserts to find a market for their merchandize. The whole display occupies nearly a quarter of an hour; and the audience extended to it the most complimentary attention; besides exhibiting some good painting, it was worked uncommonly well. The last scene, the Grove of Fate, which is changed to the Temple of Isis and Osiris, was a grand and splendid effort; and notwithstanding the immense length of this melodramatic romance, it concluded amidst the warmly expressed approbation of the audience.

DRURY LANE

The novelty at this house on Monday was an Egyptian tale of enchantment entitled "Zoroaster; or, the Spirit of the Star." The renowned Zoroaster (of this production) who is termed the High Priest of Isis and Magician of the Pyramids, was represented by Mr. Archer; and he never measured lengths in tragedy with half so much effect as he controlled Fate and "told Fortunes" in this part. Gebir, the hero of the story, was sustained by Mr. Wallack, who certainly dresses, and manages these characters uncommonly well. They are unquestionably his best efforts. Gebir is an Egyptian shepherd's son, and having received his patrimony, he sets forth to see the world. Having obtained a "wondrous gift" from Zoroaster, Gebir anon exercises his supernatural power, and straight we behold his Magic Palace and splendid Hall of

Pleasures; and the whole scene is made still more seductive and imposing by the grand Ballet of the Almehs, and the dancing of Mr. and Mrs. Noble, Mr. and Mrs. Byrne, &c. That Gebir should forget his Pamina (Mrs. W. West) amidst all this intoxicating glitter and pleasure, is hardly to be wondered at, especially as she is supposed to be of humble origin, though in reality the rightful heir of Egypt's throne. But remorse soon overtakes him:—for Pamina's right is proclaimed and her Coronation takes place. We are thence conveyed to the "centre of the earth";—Gebir becomes spellbound; we then have the following (not badly written) invocation of the Genii of the Harp (Master Edmonds, &c.):

"World let thy wonders appear at our call;
 Beauties that gem this terrestrial ball.
 Hear the spell of the harp, and appear one and all!—
 We charm thee with sounds we have caught from the spheres
 In morning's warm blushes and evening's soft tears,
 Earth's wonders and beauties be seen at our call;
 Hear the spell of the harp and appear one and all."

We next have "482 feet of powerful scenery, painted by Stanfield" displaying "Wonders of Nature and Art," and if it had been worked better, if there had not been occasion for Gebir to arise from his couch, constantly to give directions about moving it, certainly the effect on "the million" would have been still more dazzling than it was. By some fatality, the working of these matters frequently fails at this house; but as many great improvements and useful changes have taken place under the present spirited management, it is to be hoped that *this* "effect which comes by defect" may, in progress of time, be "reformed altogether." It is a matter that is devoutly to be wished, for it is an "effect defective," that sadly mars the delight prepared by excellence. In this instance, scenery (or the "Eidophusicon" as the bills term it), splendid as ever was displayed on any stage, evincing tasteful selection, bold imagination, extraordinary views, and admirable painting, passed amidst *hissing*. Besides this brilliant exhibition, we have others which rival it in grandeur and design. Ultimately Gebir, after undergoing many temptations and trials, is rewarded by Zoroaster with the hand of Pamina. On the whole, the materials of this romance are decidedly better than those which were made use of in the other house; but they are not by any means so well put together. The story and its machinery frequently move tardily, and the audience are often wearied with heavy and prosing excellence. The magic art knows nothing of stops and catches, of hesitations and interruptions, of pausing scenery or of drowsy narrative; and where they intrude, the spell is broken—the charm destroyed.

GRIMALDI'S FAREWELL

And now a Great Clown says Goodbye:

MORNING HERALD, *June 26th*, 1828 [? Author]

Grimaldi sen. had his last theatrical benefit, and made his very last theatrical bow, at this theatre last night. The house was crowded in every part; and had it been otherwise the public would have shown itself very ungrateful; for if it be true that

"Care to our coffin adds a nail no doubt,
While every grin so merry draws one out,"

then had Grimaldi a large claim on the public; for, perhaps, no man —certainly no clown—ever "drew more nails" in this way, than he has done. The entertainments selected for this occasion were Jonathan in England—in which Mr. Matthews personified his own inimitable Jonathan W. Doubikins; a Musical Mélange in which Madame Feron, Miss Fanny Ayton, Miss Love, Mr. Keeley, Mr. Harley, Mr. Morgan, and others, sung some of their best songs; the Adopted Child; the extravaganza Harlequin Hoax —in which Miss Kelly played Columbine to Mr. Harley's Harle-quin, and the whole concluded with "a selection of popular scenes from the most approved comic pantomimes"—in which the "entire pantomimic strength of the metropolis" assisted. Never was there such a concatenation of Clowns and Columbines, Harlequins and Pantaloons, as here gathered themselves together, to grace the final exit of one who was, for so many years, "the king among 'em all."—He himself performed in only one of the scenes above-mentioned—a barber's shop, from the pantomime called *The Magic Fire*; in which he played the Clown. To the performance of this part he was led on to the stage, incidentally, by Mr. Harley, in the character of Harlequin, in Harlequin Hoax, and he was received with shouts of applause. He was much affected; but, though evidently labouring under great bodily infirmity, he bore up stiffly against it and went through the scene with so much humour that the audience laughed as lustily as of old; and they were so delighted with that funny song of his about blue ruin and hot codlings, that there was a very general call for its repetition. He was too much exhausted to obey this call immediately, and eventually he was allowed to retire without repeating it. The other performances then went on, and at their close he came forward "divested of his motley" and in "good set terms," he very feelingly delivered himself thus:—"Ladies and Gentlemen; I appear before you for the last time. I need not assure you of the sad regret with which I see it; but sickness and infirmity have come upon me, and I can no longer wear the motley. Four years ago I jumped my last jump, filch'd my last custard, and ate my last sausage. I cannot describe the pleasure I felt on once more assuming my cap and bells to-night—that dress in which I have so often been made happy in your applause; and as I stripped them off, I fancied that they seemed to cleave to me. I am not so rich a man as I was when I was basking in your favour formerly, for then I had always a fowl in one pocket, and sauce for it in the other. (Laughter and applause.) I thank you for that benevolence which has brought you here, to assist your old and faithful servant in his premature decline. Eight-and-forty years have not yet passed over my head, and I am sinking fast. I now stand worse on my legs than I used to do on my head.—(A laugh.) But I suppose I am paying the penalty of the course I pursued all my life—my desire and anxiety to merit your favour has excited me to more exertion than my constitution would bear, and, like vaulting ambition, I have overleap'd myself. Ladies and Gentlemen, I must hasten to bid you farewell; but the pain I feel in doing so is assuaged by seeing before me a disproof of the old adage that favourites have no friends. Ladies and Gentlemen, may you and yours ever enjoy the blessing of health is the fervent prayer of Joseph Grimaldi—farewell—farewell"—— (Here the audience rose and cheered him loudly, with waving of hats, &c.). "Farewell," he continued—"God bless you!"

His Son, and Mr. Harley then advanced, and led him off the stage from which we may verily affirm, he retired with "all the honours."

A NEW OPERETTA

The *Tatler* takes upon itself to be very rude to Planché's new operetta. The title is *Hofer, the Tell of the Tyrol*, produced at Covent Garden:

THE TATLER, *November* 11*th*, 1830 [Hunt]

We have scarcely a word to say in favour of the opera of Hofer, The Tell of the Tyrol, which we saw last night, even though the music is by Rossini. The reader knows the story of the hero, who was an innkeeper in the Tyrol, and a brave and good man, though it is stretching a point to equalise his fame with that of Tell. Hofer did not throw off a yoke like the greater patriot. He only hindered its being changed for another, to which his countrymen had not been used. He did well to hinder their being bartered like cattle: it is only a pity that some authors who assume a right to praise him, and who do it not because he fought for liberty, but because he was a partisan of the House of Austria, do not tell us of the numberless instances in which that same house have guaranteed the same kind of transfers, and availed themselves of the iniquity. The House of Austria cut a poor figure in a story about freedom—they who are celebrated as partitioners of Poland, and despots of Italy, and who now this minute are keeping hundreds of Italian patriots in their citadels and dungeons, some of them under sentences of thirty years' imprisonment, purely for wishing to see their country independent. What would the Hofers of Lombardy say to this opera?

If there were any plot worth detailing in this piece, we would give an account of it, partly for the sake of the hero's memory. But there is none. Hofer sings a good deal, and his name is frequently mentioned. He also stalks about in a fierce hat. But he is a very melodramatic personage. The whole piece is a sort of melodrama, with Rossini's music brought to bear upon it from the opera of William Tell. A girl of the name of Bertha (Miss Pearson) is seized as a hostage by the Bavarians, because a patriot is not given up; battles take place under the auspices of Hofer; the girl escapes and joins the companions, who arm themselves and fight like the men. She has a lover (Sinclair) who vows a great deal of vengeance; divers attitudinising scenes in the mountains, with occasional pops of muskets, and marches

of soldiers, show us that the battles are going on; the patriots
get the day by dint of the usual hurras, and saying that they do;
and triumphant flags, voices and arms are raised in a concluding
chorus. We must not forget that there are dances, and that Mr.
Bland is a brave Colonel, and Mr. Webster a cowardly overseer.
One of the dances, half of peasant girls and half soldiers, has a
good effect, especially at the termination, when the military,
separating themselves on one side, gallantly lower their flags
to the females on the side opposite; though regimentals and
clattering boots do not accord with the exercise of the "light
fantastic toe." The writing of the piece is so poor that we believe
the audience did not notice a single sentence in it, with the
exception of one or two put in the mouth of Webster; and these
they laughed at, merely because they are spoken by a man in a
fright. And the verses! We will not do the author the disservice
to quote them. He would plead, perhaps, in mitigation that he
was obliged to adapt them to the music; but at least he need not
have run them out of all possible measure, so as to render them a
serious imitation of Swift's Letter of Mary the Cook. The opera is
certainly the worst of Mr. Planché's productions. The best thing
in the whole business is the scenery. There are some fine views of
Swiss villages and mountains. We do not except the music.
Rossini is a man of genius, though he has consented to pour
forth a multitude of common-places; but either Mr. Bishop has
not selected him well this time, or the music of his *William Tell*
has scarcely one touch of his genius in it, and is an enormous
specimen of his common-place. We thought the concluding line
of the first air the very best bit of composition, and almost the
only one. Like *heart* and *impart* poetry, it may be called *noise* and
destroys music. There is a prodigious quantity of clamour, of
starts and quaint passages without meaning, and heaps of notes,
such as (without exaggeration) any man acquainted with the
orchestra of a theatre might whistle all the way he went home
from Drury Lane to Paddington. There is a want of melody
throughout. If any of the airs are Tyrolean (as we believe they are),
even those are not favourable specimens of native music, but
fantastic without the beauties of fancy. Yet we must add that the
audience applauded the spectacle here and there, and seemed
unanimous in their applause when the curtain fell. The show and
the name of Rossini took them in. However, we are glad to see
they begin to think they like music.

MACREADY AS HAMLET

MACREADY BIDDING FAREWELL

To complete our disappointment, we must confess that we have not yet heard Mr. Phillips in anything which leads us to admire him as we expected to do. He is a better actor than most singers, but that is saying little; and his voice, though manly, and seconded by a correct air and taste, is too much in his throat, seeming to be invested with fat. We miss genius in him, and the power of touching the feelings. We hope we have not yet heard him in parts the most favourable to his talent. Certainly *Hofer* is favourable to nobody but the scene-painter.

KEAN ANNOUNCES HIS RETIREMENT

And now The Book grows autumnal. It is July, 1830. Kean is talking of retirement, and before that calamity all the great man's extravagances—the public discourtesies, the drunkenness, even the divorce-case—are forgotten. All hatchets are buried, and the Press is ready to believe they never existed. The scene is the King's Theatre in the Haymarket.

MORNING HERALD, *July 25th,* 1830 [? Author]

Last night, long before the opening of the doors, that part of the Haymarket fronting the King's Theatre, and the Colonnade at the back of it, were densely crowded with persons of respectable appearance, who were desirous to view, for the last time, the performances of this eminent tragedian. Shortly after the opening of the door, which, by the by, was a full twenty minutes after the time mentioned in the bills, the pit and gallery were filled almost to suffocation. In fact, the pit overflowed, and many who were compelled to take their standing on the sides of it, sought relief by getting possession of several of the lower tier of boxes, from which they were afterwards ejected, on the arrival of the parties by whom they had been taken. Although the getting in was effected with much difficulty, and there was occasionally much screaming by the females, who were seemingly very respectable, yet no accident, we believe, beyond the loss of a shoe or two, and the bruises inflicted by lean elbows on fat sides, occurred. The pit and gallery, as before stated, were overflowingly full, as were also the boxes, before the performances commenced, and the stage wings were so choked with eager spectators, as to deny to the

K

performers the privilege of ingress and egress. But amply were the audience compensated for the inconveniences incurred, by the excellence of the performances which consisted of a selection from those plays in which Mr. Kean has been most celebrated, and commenced with the fourth act of *Richard the Third*, in which Kean maintained that superiority which has ever distinguished him in this part. All his peculiar points were well made and were greatly applauded. The fourth act of the *Merchant of Venice* succeeded, and never did we hear Kean in better voice, or see him play it throughout with more decided success. The fifth act of *A New Way to Pay Old Debts* followed, which was equally successful. The second act of *Macbeth*, which contains that beautiful soliloquy, "Is this a dagger," &c. was marred by the uproarious Gods, who had an affray of their own to settle. But the great treat of the evening which was reserved as a *bonne bouche* wherewith to finish the entertainment was the third act of *Othello*, where Iago—"honest *Iago*," first impregnates his mind with jealousy. His celebrated delivery of "Farewell the tranquil mind' lost none of its original raciness (*sic*), and that harrowing speech, "If thou dost slander her and torture me," &c. was never more effectively given; it brought down a unanimous burst of applause which was repeated two or three times for the lapse of some minutes. It would be unjust, and ungallant also, were we to refrain from all notice of the ladies who gave the aid of their talents upon this occasion; but the late hour at which the performances terminated, must necessarily very much abridge our notice of them. Mrs. William West, who has been for some time a stranger to the London boards, undertook her usual part of Portia. She was warmly greeted on her entrée, and she acquitted herself with her accustomed success. Mrs. Knight, of Drury Lane Theatre, sustained the parts of Duchess of York in *Richard the Third*, and Lady Allworth in *A New Way to Pay Old Debts*, both of which she played with much judgment as did Mrs. W. Clifford in the Queen in *Richard the Third*, and Emilia in *Othello*, though in neither had she much to perform. Mrs. Bunn kindly sustained the part of Lady Macbeth, and was greatly applauded, as was also Miss Jarman, after a considerable absence from town, in the part of Desdemona. Cooper played the little of Iago which was allotted to him with great judgment. Between the acts, Messrs. Harley, Anderson and Miss Betts, sang a variety of songs which met with different degrees of success though most of them were encored.

The "Storm" by the latter gentleman, met with but a *stormy* reception.

At the conclusion of these performances Mr. Kean was led on "in the habit which he wore" as Othello, to make his farewell adieu, but the expressions of regard were of so vehement a character for some time as to deprive him if not of speech at least of the opportunity of being heard. Among other testimonials a laurel wreath was thrown upon the stage, and cries of "God bless you, Kean," "You must not leave us," and such other expressions as seemed to combine personal regard for the man with admiration for the merits of the actor. Kean possesses these in a far greater degree than any other performer, and in the latter capacity, his greatest enemy cannot deny it to him after the recent evidences which he has given at the Haymarket Theatre, which he filled to the ceiling on every night of his performance. It has been the fashion with some persons and with some actors in particular, to regard Kean's acting as humbug—that there is enough of this it must be admitted, in all professions nowadays; nor is the stage, we suspect, more exempt from it than others, where it may endure for its "season"; but will the more experienced believe that Kean's acting, if it were humbug, could retain public favour as it has done ever since he first performed in London to the present time, a period we believe of sixteen years? Attended by Messrs. Cooper and Harley, and by all who had assisted in the performance, he delivered the following farewell Address, the commencement of which he altered, adapting it to the circumstance of his enthusiastic reception, as before described:—

"Ladies and Gentlemen: You may well guess how much my feelings are corroded in the utterance of that painful word—farewell. The glorious consolation in this my, perhaps, eternal banishment, will be the recollection of your liberality and kindness on this occasion. Another point will be a solace that my mind's eye only will see—for the tears of the corporeal, I fear, would overflow my heart,—I allude to the fall of that drama, which has been the pride of Britain from the days of Queen Elizabeth to the close of our late lamented Monarch's life—Shakespeare, Massinger, Beaumont and Fletcher, and such-like names are, I understand, to be banished from the theatrical catalogue with me to make room for trans-atlantic experiments, and vaudevilles, melodramas, and second-rate music are to supply their places.

How far the British public may succumb to these innovations, would be impertinent in me to prophecy; but in the humble opinion of an honest man, whose sentiments are always undisguised, that public will soon sigh for the restoration of the legitimate drama, and blush to see the grand Temple of the Muses profaned by insignificant and ephemeral abilities. It is a national concern—the nation's honour is at stake; and as the public acts on this occasion so will the names of the present era be handed to posterity—exalted or degraded. I have no longer any individual interest in the British stage;—but in a distant country a man feels more for his own than when is a resident, and it is painful to think I shall not be able to rebut those sarcasms and vituperative invectives, when they tell me the British stage is defunct, the professors are robbed of their dignity, and the only resource the talented part of the community have left is to fly to us foreigners, and be assured of our protection. America has now become if not the cradle, certainly the bed of genius, and rewards its instructors in the histrionic art both with fortune and with friendship—a name much more congenial to the soul of talent than all the riches of the universe. But whatever events may occur, my heart will never cease to feel its attachment to its native soil; and its last pulsation will be with gratitude for its former generosity. At length I summon my resolution to my aid and that, Ladies and Gentlemen, with considerable difficulty, and with prayers and best wishes for your prosperity and happiness, and speedy restoration of your dramatic rights, I bid you a long, a last farewell."

"AN EXTRAORDINARY PERFORMER"

Now Lamb's favourite actor, Munden, leaves the stage. And even at this distance of time we feel, through Elia, a personal loss. Talfourd writes, "Lamb's relish for Munden's acting was almost a new sense. He did not compare him with the old comedians, as having common qualities with them, but regarded him as altogether of a different and original style. On the last night of his appearance Lamb was very desirous to attend, but every place in the boxes had long been secured—and Lamb was not strong enough to stand the tremendous rush, by enduring which, alone, he could hope to obtain a place in the pit—when Munden's gratitude for his exquisite praise anticipated his wish, by providing for him and Miss Lamb places in a corner of the orchestra, close to the stage. The play of the *Poor Gentleman*, in which Munden played Sir Robert Bramble, had concluded, and the audience were impatiently waiting for the farce, in which the great comedian was to delight for the last time, when my attention was suddenly called to Lamb by Miss Kelly, who sat with my party far withdrawn into the obscurity of one of the upper boxes but overlooking the radiant hollow below us, and waved to our friend. In his hand, directly beneath the line of stage-lights, glistened a huge pewter pot which he was draining, while the broad face of old Munden was seen thrust out from the door by which the musicians enter, watching the close of the draught when he might receive and hide the portentous beaker from the gaze of admiring neighbours. Some unknown benefactor had sent four pots of stout to keep up the veteran's heart during his last trial; and not able to drink them all, he bethought him of Lamb, and without considering the wonder which would be excited in the brilliant crowd who surrounded him, conveyed himself the cordial chalice to Lamb's parched lips."

The Essay entitled *On the Acting of Munden* is too well-known to quote here. Less well-known is the article entitled *Munden's Farewell,* which is not reprinted in the *Essays of Elia*:

The regular playgoers ought to put on mourning, for the king of broad comedy is dead to the drama. Alas! Munden is no more! —give sorrow vent. He may yet walk the town, pace the pavement in a seeming existence, eat, drink, and nod to his friends in all the affectation of life; but Munden, *the* Munden, Munden with the bunch of countenances, the bouquet of faces, is gone forever from the lamps, and as far as comedy is concerned, is as dead as Garrick! When an actor retires (we will put the *suicide* as mildly as possible), how many worthy persons perish with him! With Munden Sir Peter Teazle must experience a shock; Sir Robert Bramble gives up the ghost; Crack ceases to breathe. Without Munden what becomes of Dozey? Where shall we seek Jemmy Jumps? Nipperkin and a thousand of such admirable fooleries fall to nothing, and the departure, therefore, of such an actor as Munden is a dramatic calamity. On the night that this inestimable humorist took farewell of the public, he also took his benefit,—a benefit in which the public assuredly did not participate. The play was Coleman's *Poor Gentleman*, with Tom Dibdin's farce of *Past Ten o'Clock*. Reader, we all know Munden in Sir Robert Bramble and old tobacco-complexioned Dozey; we all have seen the old hearty baronet in his light sky-blue coat and genteel cocked hat, and we have all seen the weather-beaten old pensioner, dear old Dozey, tacking about the stage in that intense sea-blue livery, drunk as heart could wish, and right valorous in memory. On this night Munden seemed, like the Gladiator, "to rally life's whole energies to die;" and as we were present at this great display of his powers, and as this will be the last opportunity that will ever be afforded us to speak of this admirable performer, we shall "consecrate," as old John Buncle says, "a paragraph to him."

The house was full. *Full!* —pshaw! that's an empty word! The house was stuffed, crammed with people,—crammed from the swing-door of the pit to the back-seat in the banished *one-shilling*. A quart of audience may be said (vintner-like, may it be said) to have been squeezed into a pint of theatre. Every hearty play-going Londoner who remembered Munden years agone mustered up his courage and his money for this benefit, and middle-aged people were therefore by no means scarce. The comedy chosen for the occasion is one that travels a long way without a guard,—it is not until the third or fourth act, we think, that Sir Robert Bramble appears on the stage. When he entered, his reception was earnest, noisy, outrageous; waving of hats and handker-chiefs, deafening shouts, clamorous beating of sticks,—all the various ways in which the heart is accustomed to manifest its joy,—were had recourse to on this occasion. Mrs. Bamfield worked away with a sixpenny fan till she scudded only under bare poles. Mr. Whittington wore out the ferule of a new nine-and-sixpenny umbrella. Gratitude did great damage on the joyful occasion.

The old performer, the veteran, as he appropriately called himself in the farewell speech, was plainly overcome; he pressed his hands together, he planted one solidly on his breast, he bowed, he sidled, he cried. When the noise subsided (which it invariably does at last), the comedy proceeded, and Munden gave an ad-mirable picture of the rich, eccentric, charitable old bachelor baronet who goes about with Humphrey Dobbin at his heels and philanthropy in his heart. How crustily and yet how kindly he takes Humphrey's contradictions. How readily he puts himself into an attitude for arguing. How tenderly he gives a loose to his heart on the apprehension of Frederick's duel. In truth he played Sir Robert in his very ripest manner; and it was impossible not to feel in the very midst of pleasure regret that Munden should then be before us for the last time.

In the farce he became richer and richer. Old Dozey is a plant from Greenwich. The bronzed face and neck to match, the long curtain of a coat, the straggling white hair, the propensity, the determined attachment to grog, are all from Greenwich. Munden as Dozey seems never to have been out of action, sun, and drink. He looks (alas! he *looked*) fireproof. His face and throat were dried like a raisin, and his legs walked under the rum-and-water with all the indecision which that inestimable beverage usually inspires. It is truly tacking, not walking. He *steers* at a table, and the tide of grog now and then bears him off the point. On this night he seemed to us to be doomed to fall in action; and we therefore looked at him, as some of the "Victory's" crew are said to have gazed at Nelson, with a consciousness that his ardour and his uniform were worn for the last time. In the scene where Dozey describes a sea-fight, the actor never was greater, and he seemed the personification of an old seventy-four! His coat hung like a flag at his poop. His phiz was not a whit less highly coloured than one of those lustrous visages which generally superintend the head of a ship. There was something cumbrous, indecisive, and awful in his veerings. Once afloat, it appeared impossible for him to come to his moorings; once at anchor, it did not seem an easy thing to get him under weigh.

The time, however, came for the fall of the curtain and for the fall of Munden. The farce of the night was finished. The farce of the long forty years' play was over. He stepped forward, not as Dozey, but as Munden, and we heard him address us from the stage for the last time. He trusted—unwisely, we think—to a written paper. He *read* of "heartfelt recollections" and "indelible impressions." He stammered and he pressed his heart, and put on his spectacles, and blundered his written gratitudes, and wiped his eyes, and bowed and stood, and at last staggered away for ever. The plan of his farewell was bad, but the long life of excellence which really made his farewell pathetic overcame all defects, and the people and Joe Munden parted like lovers. Well! Farewell to the Rich Old Heart. May thy retirement be as full of repose as thy public life was full of excellence. We must all have our farewell benefits in our turn.

DEATH OF MUNDEN

Munden dies, and, with one exception, the Press is silent.

OXFORD HERALD. *February 11th*, 1832.

Poor Munden died on Monday, at his house in Bernard Street, Russell Square. He was in the 74th year of his age. Joseph Shepherd Munden was the son of a poulterer in Brook's Market, Leather Lane, Holborn; he was born in the early part of 1758. His father died when he was young, and at the age of twelve young Joe was placed in an apothecary's shop but, getting tired of physic, he took to the law. From an attorney's office he descended to a law-stationer's shop and became what is termed a "hackney-writer," to one of which fraternity in Chancery Lane he was ultimately apprenticed. He was at this time a great admirer of Garrick, whose powers he well remembered and used to dilate upon; this gave him the first inkling to be a performer. He was for some time a clerk in the office of the Town Clerk of Liverpool; but his first regular engagement on the stage was in the representation of old men, at Leatherhead. He led the actor's customary provincial round at the theatres, and soon became a partner in the Sheffield theatre. On Dec. 2, 1790, a few nights after Incledon's first appearance, Munden made his bow to the Covent Garden audience as Sir F. Gripe in *The Busybody*—and Jemmy Jumps in *The Farmer*. He was the original representative of Old Rapid, Caustic, Lazarillo (in *Two Strings to your Bow*), Nipperkin, Sir Abel Handy, and Old Dornton, besides a host not now remembered. In 1813 in consequence of a quarrel respecting the amount of his salary, he joined the Drury Lane company, making his first appearance there in Sir Abel Handy; here he remained until 31st May 1824, when he took his farewell of the public in the character of Sir Robert Bramble, in *The Poor Gentleman*. He was an excellent comic actor, and in some of his parts unrivalled—indeed, that of Old Dornton may be said to have died with him. In private life he was generally esteemed by a very numerous circle of acquaintance, not more on account of his convivial qualities than for others more substantial. A tendency to parsimony has, it is true, been objected to him as a failing; and several ludicrous anecdotes are in circulation of the skill and tact with which he not only contrived to evade a demand upon his pocket, but even to become a gainer by the attempt. The well-known story of the exchange of his old cotton umbrella for the new silk one of a friend, who requested a keepsake from him, is a case in point. In the sterling qualities which constitute the character of an honest and upright man, he was, however, by no means deficient. With respect, therefore, to his foibles, it is but just that they

> "Sleep with him in his grave,
> And not remembered in his epitaph."

NEWS ITEM

Oxford Herald, *February 11th*, 1832

A "Garrick Club," recently formed for encouragement and support of legitimate drama, opened Wednesday in King-street, Covent Garden, late Probat's Hotel—the Club consists of several Noblemen and persons of rank, dramatic writers, proprietors and Managers of Metropolitan theatres, and distinguished actors.

KEAN'S LAST APPEARANCE

"The lights burn blue." Kean is at his end.

Spectator, *March 30th*, 1833

Kean has often turned his retirement from the stage into a farce; he must now make a serious business of it. If he ever appears on the boards again, it should be only for the purpose of really bidding his admirers a last adieu. For these two or three years past, his every performance has been growing weaker and weaker, like the impressions from a fine engraving which is wearing out. Our vivid recollections, too, of his best personations when he was in his prime, have been dulled, though not obliterated, by the feebleness of his later efforts; as water thrown over the paintings on the walls of Pompeii, brought their colours out in momentary brightness, only to render them less and less apparent by each successive attempt to revivify them. He, too, must have been aware of this; and nothing, probably, but his poverty has led him to follow this impolitic course. We were not among the number of those who railed at him for so doing; admiration of his genius, and a surmise of the bitter necessity, prevented our joining in that cry. And, indeed, for our own sakes, we were even glad to see him again; with all his infirmity he was worth a score of inferior actors. He was "great in ruin." But his time is now come. His physical powers are worn out. He has at last broken down upon the boards of Covent Garden; and he only waits a fair dismissal from the scene of his former triumphs. The veteran gladiator, the victor in the arena, bows under the weight of his armour; his sword falls from his grasp, and he is borne off upon his shield.

On Monday night, brave old Kean tottered on to the stage, and presented to a pit as crowded and an audience as enthusiastic as ever thundering down applause upon his noblest efforts, his son Charles Kean, who had already been, and was now again, as warmly welcomed. The sight was one to move an old playgoer. The veteran had roused himself as for a last effort; and those who were aware of his state of extreme debility off the stage, were surprised at the eagerness almost amounting to energy, which he evinced. We never saw him personate the arduous character of Othello with more mind and feeling than he did on that night. The tone was subdued, but not a point was missed or failed. His voice sounded low and faint, but its modulations were beautiful, and responsive to the various conflicting emotions of the character. His action was feeble, yet not divested of the grace and dignity that once distinguished it. His sunken features, though their once fine outline was lost, yet seemed like the defaced fragment of some antique statue, in which might be traced the remains of its original nobleness. But we will dwell no longer upon this painful subject.

In Michael Kelly's *Reminiscences* occurs this passage:

In my humble opinion, Kean's acting in the third act of Othello, is his best performance. The first night he acted it at Drury Lane, I sat in my seat in the orchestra, which was appropriated to me, as Director of the Music, and next to me was Lord Byron, who said, "Mr. Kelly, depend upon it, this is a man of genius."